MIDLANDS BY RAIL

One thing that rapidly became apparent in planning this booklet was the enormous extent of our heritage which lies within the Midlands and also its immense diversity. There are great cathedrals, castles and historic towns but also many smaller items, often hidden away in what at first sight appear to be uninspiring urban areas, but which in fact are of absorbing interest.

We have, of course drawn attention to the well known attractions but clearly in a book of this size we cannot go into detail about them all. We have therefore tried to indicate a source from which further information can be obtained. The book, intentionally, tends to go into more detail about the smaller houses, museums and walks about which our contributors can write with personal knowledge.

This guide, then, sets out to tell you what can be seen from the train to make your journey more interesting and how to use the train to visit mediaeval castles, market towns and ultra modern shopping centres — and much more besides. A largely unknown world awaits the traveller who sets out to discover the Midlands by rail. Our authors, writing with local knowledge, will help you in that journey.

THIS IS NOT JUST ANOTHER GUIDE

IT IS WRITTEN BY PEOPLE WHO KNOW

Published by MIDLAND BRANCH OF THE
RAILWAY DEVELOPMENT SOCIETY

©MIDLAND BRANCH, RAILWAY DEVELOPMENT SOCIETY

ISBN 0 9510450 0 8

Front cover photo: Cross City line train near Gravelly Hill.

CONTENTS

RAIL SERVICE INFORMATION

The Midland Railtour ticket costs only £15 and gives 7 days unlimited travel on all the lines included in this book and more.

Details of train services and special fares are available from British Rail, Birmingham, Phone 021 643 2711.

The West Midland Travelcard is a bargain price ticket giving unlimited use of bus and rail services in the West Midland County. The ticket is valid for periods between one day and a year, the family day ticket costs £2.75, an adults' weekly Travel Card costs £5.25.

For further information on public transport in the West Midlands and Travelcards contact the West Midlands Passenger Transport Executive, Phone 021 236 8313.

EDITORS' NOTES

For some time we have suggested that if more people knew about the railways in the Midlands and the facilities they offer, there would be more passengers using them and this would be to the benefit of everyone. "Midlands by Rail" evolved from this idea and members of the Midland Branch of the Railway Development Society have therefore undertaken the not inconsiderable task of writing articles about their local lines.

We have aimed to keep the selling price low. This has inevitably led to some difficult editorial decisions. Some contributions have had to be omitted purely for reasons of space. To those authors whose articles have suffered in this way we offer our sincere apologies.

We are grateful to those members of R.D.S. who have contributed articles and to others, too numerous to mention by name, who have helped in significant ways. A special "Thank You" to Mrs. Bobby Kitson, who typed many of the manuscripts.

It is intended to produce further editions of this guide and to include some lines which have had to be excluded this time. We should be pleased, therefore, to receive comments and contributions for future editions, including photographs. They should be sent to either of the Joint Editors.

N. Cripps
98 Anstey Road
Perry Barr
Birmingham
B44 8AL

F. J. Hastilow
21 Norfolk Road
Sutton Coldfield
West Midlands
B75 6SQ

HOW TO USE THE GUIDE

This little book approaches the Midlands in terms of lines radiating from Birmingham. In a sense this is inevitable since the geographical arrangements of the railways has made Birmingham the hub of the system in the region. Nevertheless we have described many parts of the system which are remote from Birmingham. The information is there and we hope you will make use of it in your own way.

We have assumed that the reader is a passenger in a train and is sitting facing the direction of travel. An object described as on the right will then be on the reader's right hand side.

On the diagrams of lines we have used different type to indicate the relative importance of a station.

gravelly hill	is a station which is mentioned in passing
CRADLEY HEATH	is a locality which is described in more detail and has some feature worth visiting.
WORCESTER	is a place of considerable interest and has an article of its own in the guide.

All the diagrams have been printed as starting from Birmingham (with one exception — Lichfield). We felt this to be most appropriate but it does sometimes lead to the situation where North appears to be at the bottom of the diagram. Having said this we think the situation is clear enough.

LICHFIELD — BIRMINGHAM—REDDITCH

(including the Cross City Line)

LICHFIELD
|
SHENSTONE
|
blake street
|
butlers lane
|
four oaks
|
SUTTON COLDFIELD
|
wylde green
|
chester road
|
erdington
|
gravelly hill
|
ASTON
|
duddeston
|
BIRMINGHAM NEW STREET
|
five ways
|
university
|
selly oak
|
BOURNVILLE
|
KINGS NORTON
|
northfield
|
longbridge
|
BARNT GREEN
|
ALVECHURCH
|
REDDITCH

BIRMINGHAM TO LICHFIELD
(Including Cross-City North)

by Frank Hastilow

The line to Lichfield starts from New Street station which was rebuilt in the 1960s to accommodate electrification. Its shortcomings are many but it is without doubt the hub of the B.R. system, certainly as far as the Midlands are concerned and arguably of the whole system, situated as it is in the centre of the country. It is also in the centre of the city it is intended to serve — which is more than can be said of some stations! We shall almost certainly find our train — a diesel multiple unit — waiting at platform 5 from where north bound cross-city trains depart four times an hour with two continuing to Lichfield.

Almost at once after leaving the tunnel from New Street can be seen on the left the original arch at the entrance to Curzon Street station, now in use only for goods, which was the early terminus of the London and Birmingham railway. Built in the late 1830s in the Ionic style it is the counterpart of the Doric arch which used to stand at Euston at the other end of the London and Birmingham and was designed by the same architect, Hardwick. As the Euston arch has now been demolished the preservation of the one at Curzon Street takes on a greater significance. As the train approaches Proof House junction — the Proof House with its colourful crest is on the right and is still in use for testing gun barrels — one of the greatest white elephants of our time can be seen a little further away to the right. This is the viaduct built by the G.W.R. in broad gauge days, to bring their trains into Curzon Street station. Before it was completed the plan was abandoned and, apart from some small workshops sheltered by its arches, it has served no useful purpose from the day it was built.

Birmingham — Lichfield cont.

After Proof House junction our train is following the line of the oldest trunk railway in the world, the Grand Junction, completed in July, 1837, to link the London and Birmingham, not then completed, with the Liverpool and Manchester. Its terminus was at Vauxhall somewhat nearer to Proof House than the present station called **Duddeston,** (although Vauxhall still appears on the station lights).

The next station is **Aston** and here the tracks divide and our train takes the right hand branch towards Sutton while the Grand Junction continues on towards Walsall. Notice that we have now lost the overhead electric wires. After passing under the viaduct which carries the Aston Expressway, Aston church, which is well worth a visit, can be clearly seen on the left and behind it the mass of Aston Hall. Here Birmingham has retained an architectural jewel, built in the Jacobean style, which was once the manor house of the Lords of the Manor of Aston. Building was begun by Sir Thomas Holte in 1618 but it was not until 1631 that Sir Thomas was able to move in and the building was not finished until 1635. Ultimately the hall passed out of the hands of the Holte family and it is interesting to note that it was for a time leased to James Watt, the originator of the steam engine, who died there in 1848. Today the Hall is in the care of Birmingham Corporation and has recently been carefully restored and renovated. Its grounds are now a public park. It is a place well worth visiting and further information can be obtained from the City of Birmingham Art Gallery or from the Information Centre in the City Arcade.

Leaving Aston and its Hall behind the train passes the monotonous steel and concrete of Spaghetti Junction and starts the climb up **Gravelly Hill.** It passes the suburban station of that name and also **Erdington** and **Chester Road** until it reaches its highest point just short of **Wylde Green** station. A little while after leaving that station the train enters a deep cutting and, travelling fairly fast since the line is now downhill, emerges with dramatic suddenness to run onto an embankment above the rooftops of **Sutton Coldfield.** On the left, beyond the small blocks of flats, can be seen some of the 2400 acres of Sutton Park, about a quarter of which is woodland. Given to the town by Bishop Vesey under a charter dated 1528 it is now an open space which includes five pools and provides relaxation for town dwellers for miles around. The Town Gate is in Park Road and only a stone's throw from the station and, although the area around here can at times become crowded, it is always possible for those willing to walk a little way to find peace and solitude. Sutton Coldfield itself is a good shopping centre and has a number of buildings of historical interest, notably the Three Tuns Hotel in High Street — an old coaching inn, Georgian buildings in Coleshill Street and the church which dominates the town centre and which is dedicated to the Holy Trinity.

Leaving Sutton by a short tunnel our train passes stations at **Four Oaks, Butlers Lane** and **Blake Street.** This is the boundary of the County of the West Midlands and to all intents and purposes the end of the built up area as we pass at a stroke into the green of the countryside.

The next station is at **Shenstone,** a village which has developed into a small dormitory town. For those who like walking there is, near the village of Wall nearly two miles away, the site of the Roman settlement of Letocetum, much of which has been excavated and on which work is continuing. The site is owned by

Birmingham — Lichfield cont.

the National Trust and is run in conjunction with English Heritage. To reach Letocetum turn left after leaving the station, along Lynn Lane, and then take the first turning on the right, which is signposted 'Wall 2' (this rather overstates the mileage since the total distance from the station is about 1¾ miles) through the village of Chesterfield and under the modern A5 which follows for much of its way the line of the Watling Street of the Romans. Letocetum is a little further on down a road to the left but the direction is clearly indicated. The site is open in summer (March 15 to October 15th) from 9.20am to 6.30pm on weekdays and on Sundays from 2.00pm to 6.30pm but the site is closed on Mondays and alternate Tuesdays. Admission is free for members of the National Trust otherwise the cost is a modest 30p for adults and 15p for children and senior citizens and includes entry to the small museum. Incidentally it is possible to get an excellent view of the excavations from the path leading up to the church even when the site itself is closed. From Wall you can walk the couple of miles into Lichfield or retrace your steps to Shenstone station.

Lichfield Cathedral

Birmingham — Lichfield cont.

From Shenstone the next stop is **Lichfield,** the city of Dr. Johnson, whose crowning glory is its cathedral, dedicated in the 7th century to St. Chad. Its three graceful spires, known as the 'Ladies of the Vale' dominate the countryside for miles around. Apart from the cathedral the town itself is historic and well worth exploring but it is impossible to do it justice in a short article such as this. There is however an excellent Information Centre in the building next to Dr. Johnson's birthplace in Breadmarket Street to which there are clear direction signs in the city centre. Here the visitor will find what he needs to know about exploring Lichfield until it is time to rejoin his train at Lichfield City station for the return trip.

BIRMINGHAM TO REDDITCH
(including Cross-City South)

by Alan Bevan

The southern portion of the Cross-City line passes through the best scenery of all the lines radiating from Birmingham. The line has a frequent service of local trains through new and rebuilt stations to Longbridge. There is an hourly extension of the Longbridge service to the Worcestershire town of Redditch.

The former Midland Railway line to the south was the last of the major routes to be connected to New Street Station. Opened 100 years ago in July 1885 the first ½ mile is on a severe gradient through five tunnels to **Five Ways,** a station recently rebuilt and reopened after 38 years of closure. The station is adjacent to the commercial centre of Edgbaston and has heavy commuter traffic.

Shortly after Five Ways the line comes alongside the Worcester Canal (cut in 1815) and joins the route of the Birmingham West Suburban Railway which was opened in 1876 to a terminus at Granville Street, which is at the same level as the canal, between Five Ways and New Street.

Although only one mile from the city centre the railway threads a sylvan passage through the rural suburb of Edgbaston.

University — the next station was constructed for the inauguration of the cross city service and is strategically situated between the Queen Elizabeth Hospital complex on the right and Birmingham University on the left. A plaque on the station wall records the opening of this station in May 1978. From University station the discerning can visit the Barber Institute of Fine Arts to view the superb art collection during term time at Birmingham University.

After University the railway runs on an embankment which gives fine views of the Selly Oak area. Immediately before **Selly Oak** Station the railway passes over the canal and Bristol Road. The abandoned single track viaduct on the right is a reminder of the extensive rebuilding of the Birmingham West Suburban Railway when the line was doubled to become an important trunk route of the Midland Railway.

In company with the canal the railway passes alongside the world famous

Birmingham — Redditch cont.

Cadbury works at **Bournville**. Visitors who alight here can view the factory in a garden by walking along Bournville Lane away from the station, thence turning right over Bourn Brook. Ahead on the left is Bournville Carillon and to the right the village green. Beyond the green the Selly Manor and Minworth Greaves old timber framed houses are open to visitors on Tuesdays, Wednesdays and Fridays 2 - 5pm.

It is now a comparatively short ride to Lifford Curve where there is a triangular junction with the Birmingham to Gloucester Railway whose history is detailed in the Birmingham — Gloucester article.

After traversing Kings Norton junction the train enters **Kings Norton** station which has 4 platforms. The buildings near the open footbridge ahead are the original 1840 premises of the Birmingham — Gloucester Railway.

While Kings Norton became part of Birmingham in 1911 the original village centre adjacent to the station has retained its individuality becoming a significant conservation area and is worth a visit.

Leaving the station, turn right down the steep hill. Before the road begins to rise it crosses the River Rea, a somewhat undistinguished tributary of the River Tame which flows through central Birmingham in culverts. The library is on the left and the church yard on the right before the road on the right leading to the Green.

The Green is the centre of the old village conservation area. The half timbered building in the right hand corner is the former Saracens Head Inn, a fifteenth century building which was the residence of the King's Bailiff before becoming an inn. The brewery gave the property to St. Nicholas Church in 1930.

The parish church of St. Nicholas has some parts of Norman origin, the tower and spire were built five hundred years ago about the same time as the Saracens Head. To the rear of the church is another and older 14th century half timbered building known as the old Grammar School.

An inexpensive Kings Norton Trail is published by Birmingham Corporation. It is available from the Tourist Information Office in the city centre or city libraries including the one opposite the church yard in Pershore Road South.

Leaving Kings Norton station on the train there is a fine view on the left of the fifteenth century tower and spire of St. Nicholas Church which is the dominant feature of the conservation area.

The railway, now four tracked, can be observed carrying freight as well as Inter-City trains, and continues through the suburbs of **Northfield** to **Longbridge** station. Some local trains terminate here as it is the last station within the West Midlands County. The branch to the right formerly ran to Halesowen but now serves only the B.L. works, supplying components and despatching new vehicles. Ahead the sandstone rail cutting once included a two track tunnel until opened out and four tracked in 1929.

As the train emerges into the open countryside of Worcestershire we may glimpse the Upper and Lower Bittell reservoirs over the fields to the left, and admire the attractive Lickey Hills on our right. Easy and enjoyable walks over the hills can start from **Barnt Green** station where, over the footbridge and across the lane, a wide straight path leads direct to the woods and open spaces.

The main line beyond Barnt Green continues to Gloucester. However the local trains for Redditch turn off on to the sharply curved branch line platforms at Barnt Green before the tracks merge into a 5 mile long single line. Shortly after passing beneath the M42 bridge the trains meet the Worcester canal again and as we

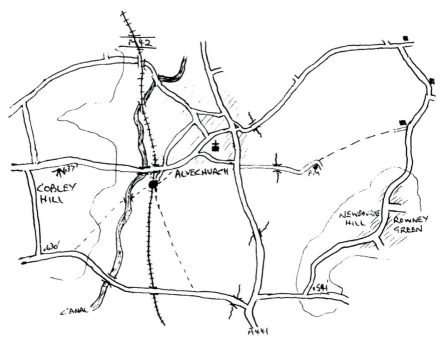

Birmingham — Redditch cont.

observe the village of **Alvechurch** our train rolls into the wayside platform complete with its station house and the original Midland Railway booking office dating from the opening of the line on 19th September 1859.

Alvechurch offers several good rambles using lanes, towpaths, or footpaths as indicated in this sketch map. From Cobley Hill (194m/630') there are splendid views southwards over the Arrow Valley towards Redditch, and westwards across the Severn Valley the distant range of the Malvern Hills can be seen.

As our train gathers speed again we cannot help but observe the large numbers of sheep grazing on both sides of the line and also admiring the lovely countryside. Entering the town of **Redditch** the line climbs and turns to reach the rail terminal. Beyond the station we can see the modern styling of the bus station and the escalators leading to the Kingfisher shopping centre. This vast indoor complex offers most of the well known big department stores and many smaller shops around an interesting central oasis with palm trees. Outdoors there is a market place and a pleasant Church Green precinct.

Redditch is of course famous for needle manufacture and the interesting National Needle Museum at Forge Mill is now open to the public from 11.30am — 4.30pm, April — October. It is the only remaining water driven needle mill in the world and has operational machinery, tea rooms, souvenir shop, Mill pool, and a picnic area. The Mill is located less than one mile from the town centre and can be reached by bus or by walking along Easemoor Road and over the main road bridge to the cross roads. If arriving by bus alight here and then turn left down Meadowhill Road which leads to the museum at the bottom of the hill. Nearby are the ruins of the 12th century Bordesley Abbey which can also be visited.

Aston Hall

Cross City train weaving through Spagetti Junction

BIRMINGHAM — CHELTENHAM — GLOUCESTER

by the editors

BIRMINGHAM NEW STREET
|
(See Cross City South)
|
KINGS NORTON
|
northfield
|
longbridge
|
BARNT GREEN
|
bromsgrove
|
CHELTENHAM
|
GLOUCESTER

The Birmingham to Gloucester Line passes through most attractive countryside as it leaves Birmingham. The Worcestershire scenery south of Bromsgrove is particularly interesting with views of the River Avon and the Malvern Hills.

An additional attraction is that the line has a frequent Inter City service with many trains operated by Inter City 125's. These trains are supplemented by local services, the principal ones being from Birmingham to Redditch and from Worcester to Gloucester.

The construction of a rail road from Birmingham to Gloucester was discussed in 1824 but the first serious proposals were made in 1832 when Isambard Kingdom Brunel surveyed a route to the east of that eventually chosen. Brunel left to become engineer to the Great Western Railway.

The route eventually opened in 1839. It was controversial in that it included the steep Lickey Incline and many shareholders thought the line should have passed through Stourbridge and Dudley rather than open countryside. It appears the railway company had insufficient money to buy anything but the cheapest agricultural land.

Most trains from Birmingham to Gloucester use the 1885 route from New Street station via Selly Oak and University to Kings Norton and Barnt Green which is described in the Birmingham—Redditch article.

Before this route opened trains from other directions had to reverse, originally at Curzon Street, and after 1854 at New Street before leaving Birmingham on the line which goes through Camp Hill, an inner suburb of the city. Paradoxically, some trains from the north west, using the newer Stour Valley route from Wolverhampton are now able to use the Camp Hill line to avoid reversing at New Street.

Trains from New Street to Leamington via Solihull and to Gloucester via the Camp Hill line follow the Leicester line while turning sharp right to join the steeply graded Camp Hill line at St. Andrews Junction, named after the church with the square tower on the right. A more famous structure named after the church is St. Andrews Stadium, the home of Birmingham City Football Club. The stadium is at the top of the cutting on the left.

After a short tunnel at Bordesley junction Leamington trains veer off to the left on a sharply curved spur to join the suburban line from Moor Street station.

Birmingham — Gloucester cont.

The Camp Hill line continues to climb before crossing the Moor Street — Leamington line and the Grand Union Canal, and on the right is a good view of Birmingham city centre. The church on the high ground on the right is Holy Trinity, Bordesley, its architecture being modelled on King's College Chapel in Cambridge. A listed building, Holy Trinity, is now used as a night shelter.

The railway passes through the suburbs of Camp Hill and Highgate before entering the tunnel at Moseley which marks the end of the significant gradients on this part of the route. After passing through the Birmingham suburb of Kings Heath the train approaches Lifford on an embankment to pass over the Birmingham—Worcester Canal just before Kings Norton junction where it joins the route from New Street via University.

The line from Kings Norton junction to Barnt Green is described in the Birmingham—Redditch article.

At Barnt Green station the Redditch line leaves to the left and the Cheltenham/Gloucester line enters a long cutting to emerge at the approach to the top of the Lickey Incline. At normal speed there is a definite "going down" sensation as the train goes over the top. In the opposite direction the ascent of the incline was once, and to a certain extent still is, a formidable obstacle to train operations. Some easing of the approaches and re-arrangement of the track now enables trains to approach the gradient at high speed.

As the train starts its descent the substantial brick building at the top of the cutting on the right is Blackwell Recovery Hospital, recently closed by the National Health Service. This was a convalescent hospital used by generations of Birmingham people.

The town of **Bromsgrove** is at the foot of the Lickey Incline. It has many interesting features but very few trains stop here. It is virtually out of the question to visit Bromsgrove by train and stay for a few hours at a convenient time. For this reason a description of the town's attractions has not been included in this guide. Bromsgrove Station is a single platform on the right, an insignificant structure for a town of this size. Immediately past the station there is an industrial belt. You will probably see some main line diesel locomotives here waiting for the call to assist a train up the Lickey Incline.

The line now passes through gently rolling countryside for the remainder of the journey to Cheltenham. Two miles from Bromsgrove the single track Worcester line diverges to the right where it meets the Birmingham-Worcester route at Droitwich. The masts on the right are the B.B.C's Droitwich radio transmitters.

The railway parallels the Birmingham-Worcester Canal first on the left and later crossing the canal which is subsequently seen from time to time on the right.

The countryside is very pleasant as the railway passes to the east of Worcester. The line crossing overhead just south of Worcester is the Cotswold line connecting Oxford to Worcester. Immediately after passing under this, the line joining on the right is used by Worcester-Cheltenham trains.

As the train begins the gentle descent to the Avon Valley the Malvern Hills can be seen on the right on a clear day.

The River Avon is crossed near Defford, the village being on the left shortly before the river. For the next few miles the railway runs through the Avon Valley, the river can be seen again after the village of Eckington.

After crossing the boundary from Worcestershire into Gloucestershire the first village of note is Ashchurch which has a distinctive Dowty factory on the right.

Cross City train near University

Montpellier Arcade, Cheltenham

Photo by courtesy of
The Heart of England
Tourist Board

Worcester

The New Inn, Gloucester

Photos by courtesy of The Heart of England Tourist Board

Birmingham — Gloucester cont.

Ashchurch, which may some day have its station re-opened, is adjacent to Tewkesbury where the River Avon joins the Severn. The square 148ft high Norman tower of the Abbey is a notable landmark. King Henry VI was slain at Tewkesbury in one of the battles of the Wars of the Roses.

The last seven miles of the journey to Cheltenham is a steady ascent. Approaching Cheltenham the Cotswold hills begin to appear on the left.

Cheltenham Station has retained much of its steam age character. The station, on a sharp curve, still has the cast iron support columns for the platform's canopy which makes an interesting introduction to a visit to this splendid Regency Spa.

CHELTENHAM

Cheltenham was an ordinary market town specialising in locally grown tobacco before waters with medicinal properties were discovered in 1761. The visit of King George III and his family in 1788 made the town fashionable but the more significant boost to its popularity came when the Duke of Wellington took the waters in 1816 and was cured of his liver disorder.

The large scale growth of the town was in the 1820's. The development utilised the Regency architectural style which has been used in Bath. There are fine examples of intricate iron work on the houses and balconies overlooking Imperial Park. Other notable buildings include the Pittville Pump Room, Town Hall, the Rotunda and Montpellier Walk.

The tourist information office is located in the Municipal offices in the Promenade which is the continuation of Montpellier Walk. The office is open from 10 a.m. to 5 p.m. weekdays, 10am to 12.30pm on Saturdays, closed on Sundays (Telephone 0242 522818).

Cheltenham is well known as a fashionable retirement and education centre. The town with a population of 73,000 is quite lively. It has an annual music festival, usually in July. This event was stimulated by the composer Gustav Holst whose birth place in Clarence Road is now a museum devoted to his life and work.

Cheltenham has the ability to turn up surprises. Perhaps it all began with the Duke of Wellington's liver! More recently the town came to prominence when trade unions were banned at a Government Communications Centre.

The station is a 15 minute walk from the town centre. There is a bus service, which runs every 15 minutes from the stop in the road outside the station. Walkers should turn right outside the station and left at the junction with the Gloucester Road. Look out on the left for the Rotunda and walk along Montpellier Walk.

The railway line from Cheltenham to Gloucester descends towards the Severn Valley. The route follows that of a tramway from the Berkeley Ship Canal to Cheltenham which was authorised by Parliament in 1809.

The line has few notable features, the Cotswold hills can be seen on the left, the M5 motorway is crossed and the Walls ice cream factory is on the left on the outskirts of Gloucester.

The train curves to the right at a triangular junction, the line joining on the left leads to Swindon and Bristol. The dominant feature of the city's skyline is the 15th century pinnacled tower of the cathedral. This is clearly seen to the left as the train leaves the triangular junction and approaches **Gloucester** station.

Gloucester

HISTORY

Gloucester is situated on the left bank of the river Severn at a spot where the crossing of the river is relatively easy. The town has grown from the Roman settlement of Glevum which was established about 96 to 98 AD and there is evidence of continuous occupation since then. A nunnery was built in 681 followed by a monastery in 821 and a Benedictine Abbey in 1022, which later became the Cathedral. There is evidence of a Castle which goes back to Norman times.

In days gone by Gloucester's prosperity was influenced for the better by the iron and charcoal of the Forest of Dean and the west of England woollen industry. The river Severn was also a useful transport route. From the 15th century Gloucester lost somewhat by the rise of Bristol.

In more modern days it has become more difficult to navigate the lower Severn. The Gloucester and Berkeley canal was built to overcome this but was not wholly successful. Today Gloucester retains some specialised traffic such as timber which is closely connected with the matchmaking industry.

RAILWAYS

Gloucester station has been completely rebuilt fairly recently. In the past trains from the Cheltenham direction bound for the South West used a loop which took them into Eastgate station whence they could continue on southwards. This station has now been closed and all trains have to use Central station which is on the line to South Wales. Consequently trains to or from the South West have either to reverse in Gloucester or miss the city altogether. It would appear that B.R. have saddled themselves with an operating difficulty which could have been avoided.

TOWN

The station is quite convenient for the town which is only a few minutes walk away. The junction of Southgate and Westgate is probably the focus of the central area. Eastgate has the city East gate with Roman and Mediaeval gate towers. This is open from May to September, Wednesdays and Fridays, 2 till 5pm and Saturdays 10am till noon and 2pm till 5pm. The Gloucester City Museum and Art Gallery is in Brunswick Road and the Folk Museum is in Westgate. Both are open all the year round from 10am to 5pm.

Gloucester docks have some spectacular early 19th century warehouses and include an Antique Centre and the Robert Opie Collection — The Package Exhibition with a selection of packaging materials through the ages. Available also are Guided Walks around historic Gloucester from June to September, taking approximately 1½ hours and departing from the Tourist Information Centre at 2.30pm.

There is much else in the way of historic streets and inns to be seen in this ancient city.

CATHEDRAL

Gloucester cathedral is situated in its quiet close to the north of Westgate. It dates back to the Benedictine Abbey which was built in 1022 and suppressed in 1539. However its church survived to become two years later the cathedral of the Diocese of Gloucester. Said to be the sixth most beautiful in Europe it is a happy combination of the Norman and Early Perpendicular styles of architecture. Many historical figures rest in this church including Robert, Duke of Normandy, eldest son of William I. There is much more of fascinating interest and beauty to be seen here than can be described in a short guide such as this.

*The Old House,
Hereford*

*Photo by courtesy of
The Heart of England
Tourist Board*

*Walking on the
Malvern Hills*

BIRMINGHAM — LEAMINGTON SPA

by Alan Bevan

BIRMINGHAM MOOR STREET
|
bordesley
|
small heath
|
TYSELEY
|
acocks green
|
olton
|
solihull
|
widney manor
|
dorridge
|
LAPWORTH
|
hatton
|
WARWICK
|
LEAMINGTON SPA

England's finest mediaeval castle at Warwick and the fashionable spa town of Leamington Spa are but two of the attractions for visitors to be found along this former main line of the famous Great Western Railway.

The route was opened in 1852 from Paddington as a 7 foot broad gauge railway and ran through a tunnel under the city centre into a station at Snow Hill. Although the tunnel has lain unused since 1972 work is now under way to re-open the rail link for commuters in 1987. The Leamington line is now served by regular local trains from the Moor Street terminus adjacent to the busy Bull Ring markets area.

Immediately after departure trains cross a 60 arch viaduct high above Digbeth, affording a wide vista of the city's tower blocks and some of the more distant suburbs. Our first call is **Bordesley** which serves St. Andrews football ground, the home of Birmingham City (Blues) which is situated on the hill top on the left hand side. Almost hidden below is the Grand Union Canal which the railway generally follows and which it crosses some four times before reaching Leamington.

Our train then passes under the Camp Hill line (see Birmingham — Cheltenham — Gloucester) and is joined by the line from New Street which is used by some Inter-City trains. We soon reach **Small Heath** which is alongside the new Small Heath by-pass road, and immediately after crossing the canal the **Tyseley** Railway Museum and depot comes into view. A number of steam engines and restored coaches can usually be seen. The Museum has several "Steam Weekends" during the year for rail buffs young and old. Further information about these can be obtained from the Birmingham Railway Museum, Warwick Road, Tyseley, Birmingham, B11 2HL. Telephone 021 707 4696. Tyseley Station (B.R.) is one of the few still retaining its full G.W.R. platform buildings and awnings.

At the junction immediately beyond Tyseley station trains to Henley in Arden take the right hand fork but the main line to Leamington takes us on via **Acocks Green,** where we again see the canal alongside on our left, and to **Olton** station, well sited amidst suburban housing. Just after the large girder bridge, laid skew across the Warwick Road, the railway runs alongside Olton Reservoir which serves sailing enthusiasts and keeps the local canal topped up.

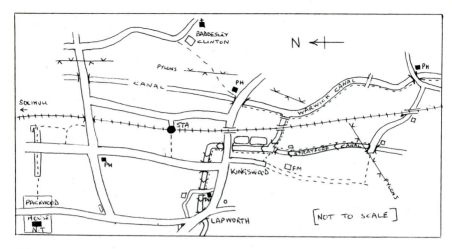

Birmingham — Leamington cont.

The next stop, **Solihull,** offers a major shopping centre in congenial surroundings. There is a large swimming pool close to the station and pleasant local parkland. Moving on, our train overlooks more rural Solihull from high embankments. After the new housing estates around **Widney Manor** station we cross the M42 and the Blyth valley. At Bentley Heath is the only level crossing on the route and our train reaches **Dorridge,** the outer terminus of some local trains. This is the last station within the West Midlands Metropolitan County.

Lapworth, the next station down the line, offers several interesting outdoor ventures in pleasant countryside. One easy journey for the whole family just two minutes away is to turn right on leaving the station, go down the lane then turn right again under the railway bridge. Here we come across the interesting locks, bridges and pools of the Stratford upon Avon canal. From here a short circular walk takes us along the towing path past the pools, over the narrow metal railed bridge and, following the canal spur, under the railway. Turn left at the canal junction back to the main road and again left to complete the circle in a mere 15 minutes.

A longer 45 minute walk takes us from the pools down the canal towpath past moored craft and quaint cottages. Just after the pylons, turn down the narrow lane on the left and continue under the railway bridge. At the "T" junction turn left and ignoring, if we can, the pleasant canalside public house continue left down to the canal tow path which will lead us directly back to Lapworth.

Also within 1½ miles of Lapworth station and easily reached on foot are both Packwood House and Baddesley Clinton Hall. Packwood is a 16th century timber framed stately home with a formal garden. It is now owned by the National Trust and is open to the public on Wednesdays and Sundays from May to September. Baddesley Clinton Hall is a "secret" moated house containing several hiding places and is also now open to the public on certain days. Both are well worth a visit.

Beyond the canal junctions the train continues through enjoyable Warwickshire countryside to **Hatton Junction** station and yet again we follow the

Warwick Castle

Photo C. Rathbone

Birmingham — Leamington cont.

Grand Union canal running on our left through a series of locks parallel to the rail line as it descends towards **Warwick**. Looking ahead we might glimpse the castle tower on the right over the town. Both castle and town centre are a mere 5 minutes from the station and the route passes St. John's House museum situated in a 15th century Jacobean mansion.

The glory of Warwick, though, is the 13th century castle, now owned and operated by Madame Tussauds. It contains an armoury, state rooms, dungeons, waxworks, riverside gardens and refreshment facilities and is open every day (except Christmas Day) from 10am to 5pm. It encompasses a thousand years of England in one glorious day's visit.

In Warwick, St. Nicholas Park, next to the river Avon, offers pleasant gardens, cafe, picnic area and boating. An interesting County Museum is situated in the Market Place which itself is alive with stalls on market days. The nearby Dolls Museum, which is open on weekdays from 10am to 5pm, is in Castle Street and the Queens Own Hussars Museum is in Lord Leycester's Hospital in Westgate.

Our final destination by rail is **Leamington Spa** which offers fine shopping facilities. Market days are Wednesdays and Saturdays. The famous Jephson Gardens include the Royal Pump Rooms, Gardens, Lawns, Lakes and Tea Rooms. Trains from Leamington Spa also serve Stratford upon Avon, Banbury, Oxford and to Birmingham New Street via Coventry.

BIRMINGHAM — HENLEY IN ARDEN — STRATFORD UPON AVON

by Simon Richards

BIRMINGHAM MOOR STREET
|
bordesley
|
small heath
|
TYSELEY
|
spring road
|
HALL GREEN
|
yardley wood
|
shirley
|
whitlocks end
|
wythall
|
earlswood
|
the lakes
|
wood end
|
danzey
|
HENLEY IN ARDEN
|
wootton wawen
|
WILMCOTE
|
STRATFORD UPON AVON

The North Warwickshire line diverges from the Birmingham — Leamington line just south of **Tyseley** and continues for 20 or so miles to Stratford upon Avon.

After leaving Tyseley, a shallow cutting is entered which takes us to the first station, **Spring Road**. The train then passes through a short tunnel, above which is the car park for the Lucas Aerospace Factory.

Hall Green is the next stop. This station is on the Birmingham Outer Circle bus route and so may be a convenient starting point for many people wishing to travel on the line. About ¾ of a mile from the station is Sarehole Mill, a fully-restored watermill, dating back to the fifteenth century. It has connections with two famous people — Matthew Boulton, who was once a tenant of the Mill and J. R. R. Tolkien who, at one time, lived close by. It is open from early April until late November between 10am and 5pm Mondays to Saturdays. Admission is only 40p for adults and it is well worth a visit, not least because it gives an insight into rural life in the area in the nineteenth century. (Now the area is far from the country).

After Hall Green, the train passes through some pleasant suburbs of Birmingham to the next station at **Yardley Wood**. Then a long, straight embankment takes it to the most important intermediate station **Shirley,** which has changed less over the years than many other stations. It still retains the original buildings on each platform,, both with canopies, a footbridge and a platform signal-box.

This is where town meets country. The railway also changes — semaphore signals replacing colour light signals. Every alternate train terminates here and most stations from here to Stratford are now unstaffed. Shortly after leaving Shirley, the railway crosses the Stratford on Avon Canal for the first of three times. After the coming of the railways, this canal, like so many others, began to deteriorate. By 1958, it was in a critical state — so bad, in fact, that the Southern Section was about to be closed. It was saved by a group of dedicated volunteers.

Birmingham — Stratford cont.

Some of the work was done by prisoners.
The next station is **Whitlocks End Halt** followed by **Wythall**. Then, after skirting Fulford Heath Golf Course, the train arrives at **Earlswood**. A hundred yards to the right of the station entrance is a path into Earlswood Woods, a starting point for some pleasant woodland walks.

After leaving Earlswood, the railway passes through the woods to the next station, **Lakes Halt,** which is characterised by a very short platform. Usually one or two fishermen can be seen leaving the train here as this station serves Earlswood Lakes. The Lakes, three in all, were originally built to feed the Stratford on Avon Canal, but are now used mainly for sailing and fishing.

Next comes a reminder that we are living in the twentieth century. The M42 Motorway, at present in an advanced stage of construction, crosses the railway before the next station which is **Wood End**. The train then enters a short tunnel, on the other side of which, the undulating countryside is delightful.

Between here and Stratford is rural Warwickshire at its best and a trip on the line is worthwhile for this reason alone.

To the right is the village of Tanworth-in-Arden. Look out for a tree-lined drive. This is the remains of the drive between the 300 year-old Umberslade Hall and Tanworth village. The railway bridge which crosses it is built from grey stone, as opposed to the blue brick of other bridges. This was done at the request of the owner of the land when the railway was built.

Danzey is the next station and this serves the village of Tanworth-in-Arden — which is a 1½ mile walk away. Tanworth, pretty and unspoiled, is the typical English village with a traditional village green surrounded by picturesque cottages, a beautiful church dating back to 1300 and an inn. The latter serves real ale and a large variety of bar food.

After Danzey, the train picks up speed as it travels down the gradient towards **Henley in Arden**. The station here is well-kept and even has colourful flower beds. Henley in Arden is an 'Olde Worlde' town and has a market on Wednesdays and Fridays. There are some fine buildings, many half-timbered, on each side of its long High Street and there is an abundance of eating and drinking establishments. You can also enjoy one of the famous Henley Ices.

Wootton Wawen station follows at the end of a long straight section. This village has the oldest church in the county. Leaving Wootton Wawen, the train takes a left-hand turn and this time passes under the canal. To the right, it is just possible to see the earthworks of another railway.

This was the Alcester branch which had an eventful history. It was closed for the first time in 1912. The track was lifted and used for military purposes during the 1914-18 war. The line was relaid and then re-opened in 1923. It was closed to passenger traffic again in 1939. During the Second World War, the Maudsley Factory moved to Great Alne from Coventry — special workers' trains were run to serve it until 1944. The line was completely closed in 1951.

Birmingham — Stratford cont.

The Leamington — Stratford line joins the North Warwickshire line at Bearley junction a few hundred yards farther on. The next station is **Wilmcote**. Mary Arden, the mother of William Shakespeare was born here and the Tudor farmhouse where she lived is open to the public all the year round. However, in winter months the admission times are limited. At Wilmcote the canal is close to the railway and it is possible to walk along the tow path to either Stratford or Wootten Wawen.

The train proceeds down the bank and soon industrial buildings replace green fields. A gas regulator is on the left and a football ground to the right. The Stratford Canal is crossed for the last time and the terminus is reached.

Stratford on Avon being the Mecca of tourism, has plenty of attractions to offer the visitor. In addition to the Shakespeare-related ones, there is a Motor Museum and a Gun Museum. The River Avon flows gently through the town and a pleasant day can be spent on or by the river. It would be impossible to do justice to the town in this limited space, but the Tourist Office, on the corner of Bridge Street and Henley Street, will provide you with all the information you need to make your visit both enjoyable and worthwhile.

Henley in Arden

BIRMINGHAM — KIDDERMINSTER — WORCESTER — HEREFORD

BIRMINGHAM NEW STREET

SMETHWICK ROLFE STREET

smethwick west

langley green

rowley regis

old hill

CRADLEY HEATH

lye

STOURBRIDGE JUNCTION

hagley

blakedown

KIDDERMINSTER

hartlebury

droitwich

WORCESTER
shrub hill & foregate street

malvern link

GREAT MALVERN

COLWALL

LEDBURY

HEREFORD

Birmingham — Worcester (via Kidderminster)
by Clive Rathbone

As do most of the excursions in this book, our journey starts from Birmingham and from New Street station, usually from platform 1B or 4B and there is one train an hour which goes through to Worcester although there are also two trains an hour as far as Stourbridge Junction, one of which continues to Kidderminster.

A description of the line as far as Galton Junction is included in the section on the Birmingham — Wolverhampton line.

Passing under the new A457 the train arrives at **Smethwick West**. Here the line from Snow Hill, soon we hope to be re-opened, comes in from the right. It is worth pausing here to look at Telford's bridge directly opposite the station, across the main road. Built in 1820 it is the second oldest iron bridge in the world, being overshadowed by its Ironbridge forebear, though it must be conceded that the earlier bridge has a more scenic location.

Pausing at the inaptly named **Langley Green** the train crosses under the M5 motorway and reaches **Rowley Regis**. Shortly after leaving Rowley Regis the train enters **Old Hill** tunnel which has a fair gradient. This helps on outward journeys but causes difficulties for the ageing d.m.u.s. in the opposite direction. Local legend has it that no less a person than Jack the Ripper visited Old Hill one foggy night in November, 1888. It came about because a man answering the Ripper's description got out of a train at Old Hill, took lodgings at a nearby pub and was found drowned the next day. There were no more murders but it should be remembered that no doctor in the country who wore a moustache was safe at that time.

Coming back to the present day, the train carries on through an urban rather than an industrial landscape to **Cradley Heath,** where a new station and bus interchange have recently been opened. For centuries the Black Country has been

Birmingham — Worcester cont.

a centre for chain making. Mostly it was a real 'cottage industry' with the chain makers and their forges operating in a workshop immediately behind the living quarters. Many of the largest chains, including anchor chains for some of our biggest ships have been made in this way. Chains are still made in the area in large factories but a small working museum, the Mushroom Green Chainshop, shows how it was done years ago, employing a mere handful of workers. The 232 bus or a short walk via Lower High Street and St. Annes Road will bring you to the Chainshop which is open daily from Easter to the end of October (but go on the first Sunday of the month if you want to see a working demonstration). Admission is free.

After leaving Cradley Heath our train pauses at **Lye** before reaching **Stourbridge Junction,** a 1920s G.W.R. station recently restored. Like many towns, Stourbridge did not want the railway on its doorstep. Realising their mistake, however, the town council took the unique step of allowing a separate railway to be built into the town. And so it is to this day that passengers for Stourbridge Town change to the little railcar that runs down to the Town station in a little over two minutes.

Stourbridge is of course renowned for its fine glassware. The works of both Webb Corbett (Brierley Hill 5281), admission 50p, and Stuart Crystal (Brierley Hill 71161), admission free, welcome visitors. Tours of the factories are available from Mondays to Fridays at various times but it is advisable to pre-book. Both firms have a 'seconds' shop where many bargains in choice glassware are to be found. Stuart Crystal have developed the Redhouse Glasscone, built in 1790 as a Glassmaking Museum, showing how glass was made 200 years ago, but you will find it has changed very little. The Glasscone is open daily between 10am and 4pm, admission here is also free. Buses nos 551, 554 or 556 will take you there from Stourbridge station.

Afterwards you may care to visit the Broadfield House Glass Museum at Kingswinford. It has exhibits of early glass making tools and artefacts. It is situated a mile further on and the same buses will take you there. The Museum is open from Tuesday to Friday from 2pm till 5pm and on Saturdays from 10am till 1pm and 2pm till 5pm. Admission is 75p for adults and 40p for children and senior citizens.

Meanwhile, back at Stourbridge Junction our train is waiting to continue its journey. On the move again it soon leaves the West Midlands County and enters Worcestershire and the scenery, which has been urban throughout, now becomes rural. The train pauses at the residential villages of **Hagley** and **Blakedown** before arriving at **Kidderminster.** Known for its carpets, Kidderminster is also the birthplace of Sir Rowland Hill, originator of the Penny Post. Without railways it is difficult to see how this could have come about as millions upon millions of letters have been carried by train since Sir Rowland's day.

The town is now a Mecca for railway enthusiasts as it is the new southern terminus of the Severn Valley Railway. Here it is possible to ride behind magnificent steam locomotives along the scenic valley of the river Severn for 14 miles to Bridgnorth in Shropshire.There you will find a mediaeval and Tudor town perched high above the river with Britain's only inland cliff railway to help you reach it. Or you might choose to visit the Georgian splendour of Bewdley with its quays on the river Severn where trading ships used to discharge their wares.

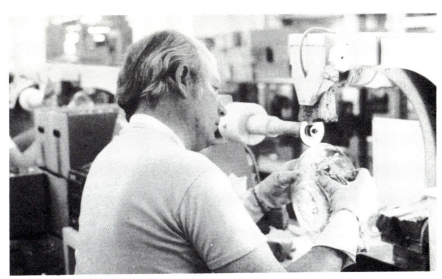

Glass cutting at Stuart Crystal

Photo C. Rathbone

Birmingham — Worcester cont.

If you prefer the tranquil side of life visit the riverside villages of Arley, Highley or Hampton Loade where time seems to have stood still. These attractive riverside locations can be reached by the Severn Valley Railway which, in addition to attracting visitors to see its steam engines also provides a public transport access to these remote places. All trains have refreshment facilities — which is more than can be said of British Rail.

If you purchase a return ticket for the entire journey on the Severn Valley Railway you can leave the train at any station on route and continue your journey on a later train. B.R. offers very cheap inclusive fares from any station in the West Midlands. Information about the times of trains etc. on the Severn Valley can be obtained from Bewdley station (Bewdley 403816).

Leaving Kidderminster the train runs alongside the Severn Valley tracks for about 1 mile, passing only the outskirts of the town as the station is some distance from the centre. It then crosses the 23 arch Kidderminster viaduct which is some 80 ft high. The scenery remains rural as the train proceeds towards **Hartlebury** where there is a castle, actually a 17th century house, part of which houses the Worcestershire County Museum. Admission to the house is 35p but the Museum is free. Both are open on Sundays, Mondays and Tuesdays between 2pm and 5pm from Easter to the end of September. Unfortunately only the trains leaving New Street at 7.02am and 7.45am stop there and the only return trains are at 5.08pm and 6.08pm and there is no service at all on Sundays or Bank Holiday Mondays!

The line from Birmingham via Bromsgrove joins immediately before **Droitwich Spa** which, as it's name suggests is an English spa town. The baths are however used solely for medicinal purposes and are not open to the general public.

The train enters a short tunnel and when it emerges we are in the approaches to **Worcester** — the "Faithful City" and away in the distance on the right can be seen

Birmingham — Worcester cont.

the outline of the Malvern Hills. After traversing the urban landscape of the city, our train negotiates a fairly sharp curve to bring us into Shrub Hill, the larger of the two Worcester stations. Here there are interchange facilities for services via the Cotswold line to Evesham, Oxford and London Paddington and in the other direction to Great Malvern, Ledbury and Hereford. The station is also served by Inter-City trains from New Street to Gloucester and the south-west. Shrub Hill station itself has much to attract those with an interest in railway architecture.

The train has to reverse to cover the final ¾ mile to Foregate Street station. This is a smaller station than Shrub Hill with fewer facilities for travellers though it can boast connections to Paddington and to the Malverns and Hereford. It is also much more conveniently situated for the centre of Worcester.

And so we have finished this part of our journey in a cathedral city 33 miles from Birmingham. It is a journey of crafts and craftsmen from the mediaeval builders of the cathedral and the porcelain makers of Worcester through the chainmakers of Cradley Heath, to the glassmakers of Stourbridge.

Severn Valley Railway train near Bewdley

Worcester

There is much to see in Worcester though the city has suffered somewhat through re-development since the war and some of the mediaeval heart of the town has been torn down to make way for modern buildings. Pride of place must be given to the cathedral which stands high above the banks of the river Severn. Construction was begun in 1084 by Bishop Wulstand. Little of this building remains above ground but the crypt survives. Constructed as a shrine to St. Oswald, this is the most remarkable feature of the architecture of Worcester cathedral.

In the body of the building the discerning eye can spot a deterioration in the quality of the stonework at the rear of the nave; improvements were half completed in the 1340s when the Black Death killed over half the citizens of Worcester, including every experienced mason, leaving only novices and apprentices to complete the task.

This great building contains the tombs of King John and Prince Arthur. The latter was the elder brother of Henry VIII and the first husband of Catherine of Aragon.

Much of the exterior stonework was replaced in Victorian times. Nevertheless the cathedral, and its close, with its many monastic buildings, provide rewarding objects of study. Worcester shares with the cathedrals of Gloucester and Hereford the hosting of the Three Choirs Festival.

The city is also famous for Royal Worcester Porcelain and the factory where it is produced is located in Severn Street, about 100 yards from the cathedral. Visits can be arranged but need to be booked well in advance by phoning Worcester 20272 and cost £1.40. The excellent museum is a feast for the eyes and shows the development of Worcester Porcelain from the plain but priceless 18th century cream jug which was the first ever piece of Worcester Porcelain. The museum is open from 10am to 5pm, Monday to Saturday while the factory is open during the same hours but only from Monday to Friday.

The city is also the heartland of Sir Edward Elgar, famous as the composer of the Pomp and Circumstance Marches, the Worcester Suite and many other works. Near the cathedral the city at last has a statue worthy of the great man, a splendid bronze work which was unveiled by Prince Charles.

Also situated close by is the Worcestershire County Cricket Club whose picturesque ground, under the shadow of the cathedral, is sited close to the river and by the same token is liable to be flooded if the river is high. All the same Test Matches are played here from time to time.

Further information about the many attractions Worcester has to offer can be obtained from the Tourist Information Office whose phone number is Worcester (0905) 23471. It is situated in the Guildhall in High Street. To reach it turn left after leaving Foregate Street station and walk 300 yards straight down Foregate Street, of which High Street is a continuation. The Guildhall is on the right and has been recently renovated.

Worcester — Hereford
by John Boynton

The Worcester to Hereford line is twenty nine miles long and full of interest. After leaving Shrub Hill station the train bears left on a sharp curve high above the city until Foregate Street is reached. Passengers joining at Foregate Street should listen for the announcements and check their train and platform thoroughly. The station is not double tracked, despite appearances, but two single tracks side by side. Thus you can leave from either platform for Worcester or Hereford, depending on whether or not your train is calling at Shrub Hill.

Across the Severn the two single railway tracks become conventional double track at Henwick, site of a former station. Commuters from this side of the city, crawling over the road bridge, probably wish it was still there! Vague moves to resurrect it in recent years and provide it with a decent car park have so far come to nought.

The train gathers speed for the seven mile sprint to Malvern Link through rolling countryside sprinkled with orchards and hop fields, the latter sheltered by very high and narrow hedges. The hop fields look their best on a sunny spring day when the bright new yellow-brown twine has just been erected for the plants to climb up. The perspective and movement of all these lines with and against each other as the train speeds by is a sudden shock to the eye. Adjacent to **Malvern Link** station is a startling new fire station, completed 1984, not actually seen to full advantage from the train but a small refreshing kick in the pants for the vast majority of boring modern buildings. The person who designed this actually cared.

Malvern Link to Great Malvern is a short uphill grind for the train, with good views of the hills to the right. The station at **Great Malvern** is the best on the line, an elegant Victorian masterpiece dating from 1863 and hardly altered since, save sadly for the demolition of the road entrance canopy and a splendid tall clock tower on the roof. The platform canopies are supported by wrought iron pillars topped with foliage and fruit picked out in the original colours. Malvern itself is a pleasant sedate town, formerly a spa, with many fine houses from the eighteenth and nineteenth centuries, a superb parish church, family run shops and a rich cultural life. The station is a pleasant ten minute walk from the town centre and the walk is all very much uphill — I learnt to drive in Malvern and, believe me, if you can do a hill start here you can do one anywhere. The parish church is a building full of interest and was once attached to Malvern Priory. When this was disbanded and demolished by Henry VIII the same fate threatened the priory's church. The townspeople were anxious to adopt it as their parish church, so hastily petitioned the king and sent him all the money they could muster, twenty pounds. In an uncharacteristic burst of generosity the king agreed, and so the Priory Church has been the parish church ever since. Just below the priory and separating it from the park is the Winter Gardens, a building looking so awful on the outside as to be beneath criticism, yet inside the facilities for plays, films, concerts, even wrestling matches are rare for a town of this size.

Leaving Great Malvern the train climbs and curves inexorably to the right as it aims for Colwall Tunnel to take it under the hills. The whole town can now be seen at its best from the train, whilst to the left the dishes on the roofs mark the Royal Radar Establishment, top secret but a major employer in the town. The other major employer, the Morgan car factory, cannot be seen from the train, though its products are much in evidence on the streets. The double track becomes single at

Worcester — Hereford cont.

Malvern Wells and as the hills draw nearer the houses on them appear more and more to cling to them and stand on top of one another. The dip in the hills above the tunnel is the Wyche Cutting, 'wyche' indicating that the spine of the hills once carried the path of one of the ancient saltways from Droitwich. Until 1974 this spine was also the boundary between Worcestershire and Herefordshire and there are still many people hereabouts, especially in Herefordshire, who still think of the one county as two separate ones and who claim that they 'worked' better that way instead of in forced harness; I agree with them.

The tunnel at Colwall is the second of the species, the first can be glimpsed through the undergrowth on the right just before the train plunges into the gloom. The original took several years of blood, sweat, tears, picks, shovels, primitive explosive, and very little else to be hewn out of some of the oldest and hardest rocks on earth. Unfortunately it was not as sound as most examples of Victorian engineering have proved to be, and when by the end of the First World War trains could be seen emerging with bits of decayed brickwork littering the carriage roofs something had to be done. A new tunnel was bored, also brick lined, and this has now served longer and better than the original. It is almost a mile long, dead straight on a rising gradient of 1 in 80, and shortly after emerging the train stops at **Colwall,** the summit of the line. On the right just before the station is the mineral water bottling plant at Colwall Springs from whence the Queen is supplied with pure Malvern Water. This pleasant village has expanded during the past ten years now that builders and estate agents have finally come to hear of its idyllic situation and its attractive train service. (It is the last remaining village in Herefordshire with a railway station). The fabric of much of the old village is there still, because the newcomers have not taken over the existing houses at ridiculous prices, but clustered into new two-garaged ghettoes of their own. The 'old' village is Victorian, coinciding with the arrival of the railway, when the Mediaeval settlement a mile away was largely abandoned, leaving the church and manor house stranded in a sea of barley fields at the end of a forgotten lane. The station is now a one platformed halt, though it must surely remain the smallest station in Britain with a public address system, which has been operating since the station lost its staff in 1969. Intending passengers are informed of the running of trains by the signalman at Ledbury, and the loudspeaker is slung underneath the footbridge which carries a path to some attractive walks in the woods above the village.

Leaving Colwall the hills are now on the left and it is obvious that one of them has man made earthworks at the summit. This is British Camp or the Herefordshire Beacon, and the ramparts are supposed to date back to the Iron Age. It is one of the alleged sites of the last stand of Caractacus against the Romans. The railway now falls away, a shallow cutting deepens and a gentle curve sharpens as the train enters Ledbury tunnel. It is dead straight except for the first few yards, and is slightly shorter than Colwall tunnel but it is unlined and has a much narrower bore.

Ledbury station is very near the tunnel mouth and here the track is double again. At the time of writing it remains double all the way to Hereford, but there are plans to single this stretch and just keep Ledbury as a passing loop. This would impair the flexibility of the train service and restrict alterations and improvements in the future. The lesson of too much single track has not been

Worcester — Hereford cont.

learnt from the Cotswold line, between Worcester and Oxford, singled for long stretches in 1969 and operating in something of a straitjacket ever since. The town of Ledbury, a level half mile walk from the station is very handsome. Although much visited by tourists it is not a museum piece littered with antique shops and bogus tea shoppes à là Broadway. The walk up Church Lane to the parish church is the nearest we can get in any town anywhere to walking up a genuine intact Mediaeval alley, minus the smells and squalor. The church itself is well proportioned and light and airy inside, with a huge modern crystal cross hanging above the altar. The steeple tower is detached from the rest of the building, a characteristic of some other good Herefordshire churches. At the foot of Church Lane is the Buttermarket, one of the best stilted market halls still used for its original purpose. Ledbury's most famous son was John Masefield, the former Poet Laureate.

Leaving Ledbury the train crosses the high red-bricked Ledbury viaduct, completing the line's tally of major works — two tunnels and two viaducts. As speed increases hop fields and cider apple orchards predominate and the soil is very much redder now. Then comes marshy pasture, prone to flooding, which is the valley of the Lugg, a tributary of the Wye.

Hereford
by E. W. Robinson

As the railway line from Worcester approached Hereford it joins the old Shrewsbury and Hereford Joint Railway (opened in 1853) and the train travels over that line for 1.5 miles to Barrs Court station. Rounding the curve past Brecon Curve there is a fine panorama of the city with the towers and spires of the cathedral and other churches.

The city of Hereford was established in the dark ages to guard the ford over the river Wye. It has a turbulent past including raids by the Welsh and finally a siege by the Scots during the Civil War. Owen Tudor was beheaded here and Nelson visited it. Nell Gwynne and David Garrick were natives. Now it is mainly occupied with agriculture, cider making and some engineering.

To reach the main part of the town from the station, turn right at the end of the station approach. Proceed up Commercial Road and Commercial Street to the High Town, passing on the way the bus station and a bingo hall which have been built on the site of the County Gaol.

At the eastern end of High Town is a fine Jackson black and white house. This is the "Old House" built in 1621 and once part of "Butchers' Row".

Most visitors now go to the Cathedral, which is reached via a passageway and a narrow street called "Church Street". It is a cruciform building dating from the 11th century. The Norman arches of the nave are very fine and there is an Early English Lady Chapel with nice stained glass. The cathedral has one of the best chained libraries in the world and the "Mappa Mundi", a map of the world drawn about 1300.

Other interesting ecclesiastical buildings are the churches of All Saints and St. Peter's. The former also has a small chained library.

Leaving the cathedral at the West end, proceed down Gwynne Street where one of the buildings bears a plaque indicating the site of Nell Gwynne's birth-

Hereford cont.

place. At the end of the street is the Wye bridge dating from 1490. One of the arches is different from the others as it was broken down in the siege. In recent years a new bridge, Greyfriars, has been built upstream.

A pleasant walk can be taken from the Wye bridge to the Castle Green by way of the South Bank and the Victoria suspension bridge. In the Green are the remains of the earthworks of the castle and a pillar commemorating Nelson's victories. This was built following his visit in 1802.

HEREFORD–CITY CENTRE

Key: 1-Railway Station; 2-Bus Station; 3-Livestock Market; 4-St. Peter's Church; 5-Cider Museum; 6-Railway Centre; 7-Tourist Information Centre; 8-Library and Museum; 9-Cathedral; 10-Castle Green; 11-Wye Bridge; 12-Water Works Museum; 13-Bishops Meadow

**RAILWAYS IN
THE MIDLANDS**

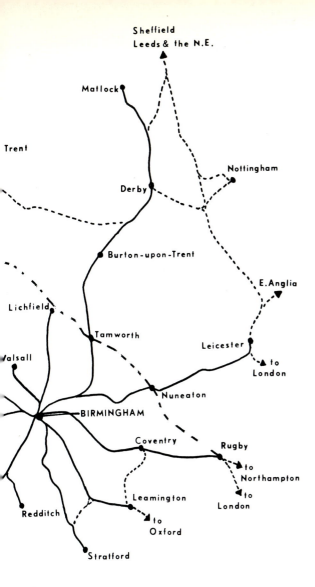

Sheffield
Leeds & the N.E.

Matlock

Trent

Nottingham

Derby

Burton-upon-Trent

E. Anglia

Lichfield

Tamworth

Leicester

Walsall

to London

Nuneaton

BIRMINGHAM

Coventry

Rugby

to Northampton

to London

Leamington

Redditch

to Oxford

Stratford

rd

——— Routes included in guide
----- Routes not included in guide   ISk

ltenham

er

d

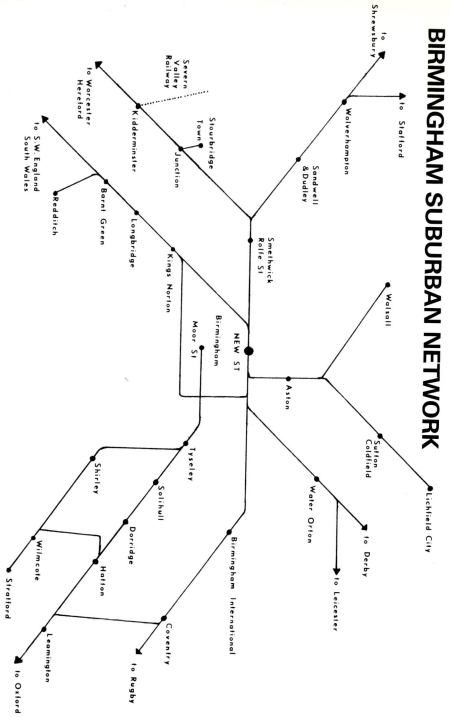

BIRMINGHAM SUBURBAN NETWORK

Hereford cont.

Returning to the cathedral by way of Castle Street some interesting Georgian houses can be seen. Other historical items of interest are portions of the 13th century walls (in Victoria Street and Newmarket Street with a bastion by the approach to Greyfriars bridge); Coningsby Hospital in Widemarsh Street which was formerly a hospice of the Knights of St. John and the adjoining ruins of Blackfriars Priory.

There are three museums in Hereford devoted to various aspects of Industrial Archaeology. They are the Herefordshire Waterworks Museum at Broomy Hill (Enquiries: Hereford (0432) 4104); The Museum of Cider, Bulmers Cider Works, off Whitecross Road (Enquiries: (0432) 54207) and Bulmers Railway Centre, also off Whitecross Road and with the same phone number for enquiries.

Other places of interest are the City Museum and Art Gallery in Broad Street and the Churchill Gardens Museum on Aylestone Hill.

Further information can be obtained from the Tourist Information Centre in the Shirehall (phone: (0432) 268430).

GENERAL NOTES ABOUT THE RAIL SERVICE

The service along this line has improved considerably in recent years. No trains on the line venture beyond Hereford, but at the other end most travel beyond Worcester to offer through trains to/from Birmingham, Oxford and Paddington. There are a few trains which do not go west of Great Malvern. Weekday services operate from around 06.30 to around 21.00. All trains call at all stations, and passengers joining at Colwall and Ledbury, which are not staffed, can buy a wide range of tickets from the guard. On Sundays the line does not open until early afternoon and Foregate Street is closed to trains, even though the travel centre is open!! Refreshment rooms are operated by British Rail Travellers Fare at Worcester Shrub Hill and Hereford and privately at Great Malvern.

RAIL CONNECTIONS AT WORCESTER

The hourly fast service between Birmingham and Worcester is a through service to Great Malvern, with alternate trains going through to Hereford. There are about eight trains each way between Worcester and Oxford, those that are not through trains to Hereford generally have good connections at Worcester. The service from Worcester south to Cheltenham, Gloucester and Bristol can be summed up in one word — appalling. It is very infrequent and most trains do not even pretend to connect with any others.

Notes cont.

RAIL CONNECTIONS AT HEREFORD

The other rail service operating from Hereford is the one between Cardiff and Crewe. There are only six trains each way per day, but they are locomotive hauled and generally offer good connections at Hereford to the Worcester line.

SELECTED WALKS

Apart from the attractions in the cities at either end of the line the best walks are to be had from Great Malvern. These all involve a stiff walk up through the town onto the hills where the views are magnificent and the paths numerous. Best advice is to take an O.S. map or buy a guide in the town. In summer the cafe on the summit of the highest hill, Worcestershire Beacon (1394ft.) does a roaring trade and even if you prefer solitude — easily obtainable elsewhere on these hills — the views from this point are worth sharing. It is possible to descend from here to West Malvern and thence through woods to Colwall, but I do not give precise directions here as such secluded and beautiful tracts deserve only to be discovered by those who are keen and armed with a map.

SUGGESTED CYCLE RIDE

Bicycles are carried free of charge on the Worcester — Hereford line, except on the solitary High Speed Train. All you need is a good map, time, good calf muscles and efficient brakes, for this is hilly country, and the cycle journey described is not recommended for children under about the age of twelve, nor for anyone who has done no cycling for some time. The journey begins at Ledbury. From the town centre the Worcester road leads to the hill at British Camp and quiet lanes parallel this route for most of the way. At the British Camp Hotel turn left along Jubilee Drive, constructed in 1897, for a superb level ride along the west side of the hills to the Wyche Cutting. Here it is possible to bear sharp left and go down into Colwall, go through the cutting and descend to Great Malvern, or best of all keep on the west side of the hills to West Malvern and North Malvern, following the road round the north end of the range until it regains the main road to Worcester, from which point it is less than half a mile of gentle downhill coasting to Malvern Link station on the left hand side of this main road. Such a ride should be done 'at leisure', with frequent stops to admire the view, regain breath and take refreshment, and would take half a day to savour fully.

This article is not intended to be a fully comprehensive guide to the places mentioned along the Worcester to Hereford line; I have merely scratched the surface and hopefully whetted the appetite. Accurate up-to-date information about the opening times etc. of places mentioned can best be obtained from the local tourist information offices before travelling. Their telephone numbers are as follows: Worcester (0905) 23471; Malvern (06845) 61896; Ledbury (0531) 2585; Hereford (0432) 68430. Information about rail travel along the line can be obtained from British Rail at Worcester Shrub Hill (0905) 27211 and at Hereford (0432) 266534.

BIRMINGHAM — COVENTRY — RUGBY

by Ian Kempton

BIRMINGHAM NEW STREET
|
adderley park
|
STECHFORD
|
lea hall
|
marston green
|
BIRMINGHAM INTERNATIONAL
|
berkswell
|
tile hill
|
canley
|
COVENTRY
|
RUGBY

The Birmingham — Coventry — Rugby line is part of the main electrified Inter-City route to London. It has a frequent service of local and Inter-City trains to Coventry, but only one train per hour calls at Rugby.

Following departure from New Street the train passes through a short tunnel before climbing to a viaduct overlooking, on the left, the site of the original London — Birmingham Railway terminus known as Curzon Street station. The original site has been redeveloped but the recently restored Ionic style original station entrance remains and is clearly visible.

Adjacent to the Curzon Street station site the train traverses a series of junctions and joins the original route of the London — Birmingham Railway. The Lichfield and Walsall routes pass overhead before heading off to the left. This railway was opened in 1838, one of the earliest trunk routes. The engineer was the immortal Robert Stephenson who designed a railway with very easy gradients.

There are views of the Freightliner Terminal and Inland Port to the left before the first suburban station **Adderley Park,** but be careful if getting off here, its platforms are very short! The line now passes through a succession of houses, factories and allotments, to the next station at **Stechford.**

This is a convenient starting point for a visit to Blakesley Hall, a recently restored 16th century timber framed Yeomans House. The hall is located in Blakesley Road, Yardley, about one mile from the station. Turn left on leaving the station and turn right at the main road (Station Road). The No. 11C Outer Circle bus provides a frequent service along Station Road. The bus stop is on the opposite side of the road. Either use the 11C bus or walk along Station Road to Blakesley Road. Turn right at the junction, the hall is located in pleasant grounds. Birmingham Museum and Art Gallery administer the property, phone 021 783 2193 for information.

Leaving Stechford the railway continues past houses and factories and the next station, **Lea Hall,** before the first view of Birmingham Airport on the right just before approaching **Marston Green** local station. Shortly afterwards, first on your right, then on the left, the housing suddenly drops away to reveal fields and one of the airport runways on the right.

Inter City train near Adderley Park

Birmingham — Rugby cont.

The train now pulls into **Birmingham International,** an Inter-City station recently built to serve The National Exhibition Centre on the left and the new airport complex. The Airport terminal which is 600 yards away is linked to the station by Maglev, a revolutionary magnetic train which hovers above its rails giving a quiet and smooth ride. It is well worthwhile riding on Maglev to the Airport Buildings and viewing the aircraft (small charge) or sampling the excellent catering facilities.

The National Motorcycle Museum is located at the M42/A435 intersection. Standing at the station's main exit the museum is to the left at the end of the access road which climbs to the motorway intersection. This modern, privately owned museum, has over 400 machines on view from the 60 year history of the now virtually extinct British Motorcycle Industry. Before leaving Birmingham International it is interesting to reflect upon how quickly this area has developed in the last 10 years from a green field site.

The train now passes through the Green Belt between Birmingham and Coventry. There are two local stations on this stretch, **Hampton in Arden** and **Berkswell,** the latter serving the village of Balsall Common. After Berkswell the train passes into a cutting signalling the approach of Beechwood Tunnel.

A few yards out of the tunnel and our brief glimpse of the countryside has gone, the train is approaching Tile Hill, the first local station in Coventry. The station has been modernised with a large car park popular for Birmingham bound commuters. The train now passes between factories on the left and on the right is

Birmingham — Rugby cont.

a combination of industry and large housing estates which are separated by public open spaces. **Canley** is next, a pleasant local station overlooked by the B.L. assembly works, formerly Standard Triumph motor cars.

The train now passes through terraced housing until entering the Inter-City station of **Coventry**. The station was rebuilt when this line was electrified in 1966.

COVENTRY

Coventry is now overshadowed by Birmingham. In 1400 this was not the case because Coventry with York, Bristol and Plymouth was one of the leading provincial centres. The city was a Parliamentary stronghold during the Civil War, the phrase 'Sent to Coventry' dates from this period because local Royalist prisoners were 'Sent to Coventry' Gaol.

The City Centre was devastated by bombing in 1940 and the Cathedral is regarded as a symbol of reconciliation as the new building rises alongside the ruins of the old.

A map outside the station shows the city centre is under a mile away along a pedestrian walkway. An alternative to walking is to ride on the No. 25 bus which departs from outside the station every 10 minutes Monday-Saturday until 1800 hours and less frequently in the evening and on Sundays. The fare is 10p any distance, adult or child. Go as far as Broadgate for the Shopping Precinct and the Information Centre. The terminus of the shuttle bus is the Pool Meadow Bus Station. The Cathedrals are 50 yards from the Pool Meadow Bus Station, no visit to Coventry is complete without looking at these magnificent buildings — the one now ruined is a reminder of the horrors of war.

Also near the bus station is The British Museum of Road Transport. Take the road on the right hand side of the Apollo Theatre and the museum is at the top of the hill in Cook Street.

While in Coventry you may also want to look at some of its lesser known attractions which survived the bombing. Firstly Fords Hospital dating back to the 16th century; this is in Friar Lane off Broadgate. Secondly St. Mary's Guildhall alongside the Old Cathedral. This contains a 600 year old guild chair and a tapestry from c1490. The Guildhall is open May-September Monday-Saturday 10.30 to 12.00 and 13.00 to 17.30; Sunday 12.00 to 17.30 — the Information Centre will give directions to both.

The footpath which passes between the new and old cathedrals leads to Broadgate. Holy Trinity Church in Broadgate is the main parish church; it has many surviving mediaeval features including a timber ceiling. The church is open the usual hours, Monday-Saturday except when there are services.

A prominent feature of Broadgate is a statue of the 11th century Coventry heroine Lady Godiva. There is an adjacent clock which on the hour re-enacts the Lady's horse ride naked through the streets, featuring Peeping Tom, the mid 17th century addition to the tale.

Coventry, along with Leamington, is the rail head for The National Agricultural Centre at Stoneleigh. Buses run from Warwick Road which is reached by a signposted footpath by the side of the station multistorey car park; special buses run from both rail heads during exhibitions and shows, otherwise catch the X6/ (infrequent — every two hours) or the 568 (also infrequent). The special buses when operating run far more frequently — for details contact Midland Red South on Coventry (0203) 553737.

Birmingham — Rugby cont.

COVENTRY — RUGBY

Leaving Coventry the train passes through another couple of miles of Coventry before breaking out into the country again. The River Avon can be seen occasionally to the left, a smaller river than when it flows through Stratford. The train takes less than ten minutes to pass through this hilly and pleasant countryside. Approaching Rugby the up line rises onto a viaduct over the West Coast Main Line before joining that line for the last few yards of the journey.

Rugby has a large station, older than those we have passed through. Those who get off here will find a smaller town than Coventry or Birmingham, one without an air-conditioned shopping centre or precinct and many will prefer this. An open air market is held several days a week, there is also a small indoor market next to it.

Rugby's principal landmark is its public school where Dr. Arnold (1795-1842) was headmaster. The game of Rugby Football was invented here when in 1823 William Webb Ellis carried the ball instead of kicking it during a soccer match.

BIRMINGHAM — WOLVERHAMPTON

by Nigel Cripps

BIRMINGHAM NEW STREET
|
SMETHWICK ROLFE STREET
|
sandwell and dudley
|
dudley port
|
TIPTON
|
coseley
|
WOLVERHAMPTON

Travelling along the electrified Birmingham — Wolverhampton line provides a fascinating kaleidoscope of 200 years of industrial history with a surprising number of outstanding features. The line has an hourly weekday local service and a more frequent Inter-City service which also operates on Sundays.

A few years ago a journey from Birmingham to Wolverhampton was a progression through a smokey industrial area known as the Black Country. The march of time has seen many major industries close. The line side is becoming green as derelict industrial sites are being landscaped by the West Midlands County Council, also Clean Air Acts have helped to reduce pollution from those factories still operating.

On leaving New Street Station the train immediately plunges into an 845 yard tunnel as it begins its journey on the Stour Valley line opened in 1852; the engineer was Robert Stephenson.

Viewed from the train it is easy to see that Birmingham has more canals than Venice. The railway parallels the Birmingham Canal Navigation (BCN) Birmingham — Wolverhampton main canal which is first seen on the left. Note the 19th century cast iron bridges, an essential feature of canal tow paths during the horse drawn era.

Birmingham — Wolverhampton cont.

After passing through a cutting, on the right is a grassed area once occupied by slum property. The dominant building here is Winson Green Gaol. It looks difficult to get into, but as the Great Train robber Ronald Biggs discovered it is not so difficult to leave unofficially if you are really determined.

The train now passes on the right, Soho Junction. This is a triangular junction with a line which joins the Walsall line near Perry Barr. Immediately after the second junction on the right is the site of Soho Foundry opened by Matthew Boulton in 1762 to manufacture James Watt's steam engines. The site is now owned by W. T. Avery Ltd. There is a small museum which is principally devoted to weighing machines manufactured by Avery's but does include some small items from the Boulton era.

Some of the original buildings remain including a cottage once occupied by William Murdoch. Murdoch was associated with Soho Foundry for 53 years from 1777 to 1830 and for some time had the task of looking after the first steam pumping engines in Cornwall. He was also the inventor of coal gas lighting.

Smethwick Rolfe Street, the first station, is conveniently located for the High Street shopping area. All the buildings on the railway side of the High Street were demolished for a new road, those remaining have recently received a facelift and present an interesting and varied vista.

It is well worth leaving the train at Rolfe Street to explore the canal and walk to W. T. Avery's museum mentioned above. Turn right on leaving the station then immediately left into North Western Road, on the right there are several points of access to the canal. First walk towards Birmingham and inspect the splendid Telford aqueduct which spans the lower canal, then continue walking in this direction past the junction of the two canals to the next bridge at Rabone Lane. Turn left into Rabone Lane, Foundry Lane is to the right and W. T. Avery's Foundry is in Foundry Lane opposite the park. The distance from Rolfe Street station is just under a mile.

Matthew Boulton's Soho Foundry still has its impressive portico. This was the greatest factory in the neighbourhood and Boulton well knew the value of the building as an advertisement. Every distinguished visitor to Birmingham wished to call there. Visitors can call at the museum by appointment, usually on Wednesdays and Thursdays. Telephone 021 558 1112.

If you are not visiting the Soho Foundry and Avery Museum turn round at the aqueduct and return to the point of entry to the canal, then continue walking into the spectacular Galton Valley cutting on the lower canal. As a minimum walk the ¼ mile to Galton Bridge or preferably continue for 1 mile past the Motorway and Spon Lane canal junction to the next road bridge. Leaving the canal turn left into Bromford Lane and you will find Sandwell and Dudley Station a short distance away on the left.

Continuing on the train from Smethwick Rolfe Street the railway runs alongside the canal which is seen on the right. Two canals are clearly visible and there are the remains of a third. The original 1772 Brindley canal was at the highest level on the far right; this is now a footpath. The higher of the remaining canals is the 1787 Smeaton improvement which eliminated some locks and overcame problems of water shortage. The lower canal was one of the numerous improvements by Thomas Telford in 1824-9 which reduced the canal distance from Birmingham to Wolverhampton by 7 miles. The steep sided cutting of the Telford canal is most impressive, especially when it is remembered that it was dug

Birmingham — Wolverhampton cont.

entirely by hand.

The brick built engine house between the two canals has just been renovated by the West Midland County Council Task Force and may one day become a museum. The engine house was constructed in 1892 to pump 200 lockfulls of water per day from the Telford to the Smeaton canal. All the machinery in the pump house has been scrapped. However an earlier pump engine which it replaced and which was located on an adjacent site is a spectacular survivor. This 1779 Watt engine has been reconstructed in working order in Birmingham Museum of Science and Industry.

Immediately before the new motorway feeder road bridge, the Stourbridge — Worcester line leads off to the left. This new bridge obscures the view of Galton Bridge, an elegant iron structure built by Telford in 1829, with a span of 150 feet and a height of 70 feet from canal to road. At the time of its construction Galton Bridge was the largest canal bridge in the world.

As the train leaves Galton Valley the M5 motorway is seen on the right. Such are the meanderings of this form of transport that the traffic running alongside the north bound train is heading south.

Sandwell & Dudley is an Inter City park and ride station. Originally and appropriately called Oldbury, because that is where the station is located, the new name is misleading. The station is in Sandwell Metropolitan District but there is no town or designated centre of Sandwell. Dudley on the other hand is both Metropolitan District and Town. If you wish to visit Dudley then stay on the local train, the centre is more conveniently reached from Dudley Port or Tipton stations.

Shortly after leaving Sandwell and Dudley the railway crosses over the canal. On the left, after the oil terminal, on a clear day Dudley town centre can be seen on a hill slightly forward of the train. In the trees the 13th century Dudley Castle in the grounds of the famous zoo will be noticed.

Dudley Port is the next station. As yet we have not reached the nearest station to Dudley although some passengers prefer to leave the train here. To reach the town cross the road outside the station and board the frequent 74 bus service into Dudley which terminates in the town centre. Alight by the bus depot for the zoo and castle.

Tipton, the next station, is only a mile from Dudley town centre, and the route to the centre passes the town's main attractions which are the Black Country Museum and the zoo which is located in the grounds of the castle.

The Black Country Museum is just over ½ mile from Tipton station. The 244, 262 and 301 bus services operate every 15 minutes and stop on the opposite side of the road to the station entrance. Before reaching Dudley town centre the buses call at the museum and zoo. Those preferring to walk should turn right into Owen Street, continue straight ahead at the first major junction and walk the length of High Street to Dudley Road. Turn left into Dudley Road, cross the busy dual carriageway Birmingham New Road and the museum entrance is in Tipton Road on the right hand side.

The Black Country Museum has a tramcar in which visitors can ride to the main exhibition area. There is a canal narrow boat repair yard and numerous exhibits showing traditional Black Country industries in reconstructed buildings. Many crafts such as chainmaking are frequently demonstrated. New buildings are

Birmingham — Wolverhampton cont.

being added continually and a visit can be a fascinating experience. The museum is open daily from 10am to 4pm but closes a little earlier in the winter. For further details phone 021 551 9643 and there is a charge for admission.

About 600 yards from the Black Country Museum is the entrance to Dudley Zoo. Continue along Tipton Road, turn right at the traffic lights opposite the bus depot and the entrance is in Castle Hill Road over the railway bridge on the right.

Dudley Zoo is open Monday to Saturday 9am to 4.30pm, Sundays 10am to 4.30pm, in winter there is an earlier closing time. Dudley Castle is located within the zoo grounds and can be easily reached by a chairlift adjacent to the main gate, for further information telephone Dudley 52401. There is an admission charge.

From Tipton the train runs through a residential area to **Coseley** station. Shortly after leaving Coseley the train passes on the right the site of Bilston Steel Works. Once an important source of employment and pollution, the area is now a notable waste site waiting for redevelopment.

The train is approaching Wolverhampton where there is evidence of active industries. To the left are the colourful gas holders of the British Oxygen Co., on the right is a steel terminal and as the train curves into Wolverhampton immediately below the viaduct there is a traditional sand foundry. From these buildings on the left the distinctive smell of the foundry industry will often enter the coach.

Wolverhampton has an attractive shopping centre within easy walking distance of the station. At the traffic lights at the end of the station drive cross straight ahead past the Grand Theatre into Lichfield Street. The shopping centre is past the next set of traffic lights on the left hand side.

WOLVERHAMPTON — SHREWSBURY

by Ian Jenkins

WOLVERHAMPTON
|
bilbrook
|
codsall
|
ALBRIGHTON
|
COSFORD
|
shifnal
|
oakengates
|
WELLINGTON
|
SHREWSBURY

The journey to the attractive county town of Shrewsbury is principally through rural Shropshire. The line gives access to one of the country's leading aircraft museums as well as the Severn Gorge, where the Industrial Revolution began.

On weekdays, there is an hourly local service, supplemented by Inter-City trains from London Euston. These usually terminate at Shrewsbury, though a few continue to Chester or Aberystwyth. On Sunday the service is much more limited.

The early history of the railway from Wolverhampton to Shrewsbury is full of intrigue, Parliamentary enquiries and violence! The result of all this difficulty was the opening of two adjacent stations in Wolverhampton, which for many years caused inconvenience to passengers. Matters

Wolverhampton — Shrewsbury cont.

have now been improved with the concentration of all services at the rebuilt High Level Station, which was the closer of the two to the town centre.

Leaving Wolverhampton, Shrewsbury trains travel a short distance along the electrified main line to Stafford. During this section of the journey, one can see an attractively landscaped canal basin and the remains of transhipment facilities for transferring goods, which had come by rail from Shrewsbury, onto canal boats. In 1850 this was the site of a serious riot, when 300 navvies, employed by the London & North-Western Railway Company confronted a similar group working for the Shrewsbury Line. After the Local Mayor read the Riot Act and troops intervened the matter was settled by a court injunction.

At Cannock road Junction the line bears left as it leaves the Stafford line, and soon joins the former Great Western main line curving in from the right. Nowadays this line chiefly carries coal traffic. The train crosses Dunstall Park Viaduct, high above the race course, before Oxley carriage sidings come into view on the left. It is interesting to note that this short length of track over the viaduct is the only part of the former Great Western Railway system to be electrified at present. (It is for operating convenience, to allow electric locomotives access to the carriage sidings).

The railway climbs a long, straight bank to its first station, **Bilbrook,** with its staggered platforms, then on just half a mile to **Codsall.** The lineside fields are scattered with oak trees, and we are reminded that it was near here, at Boscobel, that King Charles II escaped from his pursuers by hiding in an oak tree. Boscobel House, where the monarch slept after the Battle of Worcester, in September 1651, is open to the public every day except Monday. The building is in the hands of the Department of the Environment, and is a good 45 minute walk from **Albrighton,** which is our next station.

The wooden platformed station at **Cosford** is alongside an R.A.F. airfield, home of the famous indoor athletics stadium where national and international competitions are held. Also close by is the Aerospace Museum which contains a fascinating collection of Lancaster and Liberator bombers, Comet and Trident airliners, balloons, missiles, and much more. Currently the museum is open daily during the summer but closed at weekends during the winter. Through tickets at reduced fares and including admission to the Aerospace Museum are available from Coventry, Birmingham International, Birmingham New Street, Sandwell and Dudley and Wolverhampton stations.

The line is at its loveliest between Cosford and the next station, Shifnal. Trains cross richly wooded valleys, run along fern covered embankments until, at the approach to Shifnal this changes to rather more desolate land where, due to modern farming methods, many of the hedgerows have been grubbed out. **Shifnal** is a fine little town with a 12th century parish church and a street full of half-timbered buildings, a considerable number of which seem to be pubs!
There is a steep ascent from Shifnal to Madeley Junction, where a freight only

Wolverhampton — Shrewsbury cont.

line heads off (left) to serve Buildwas Power Station. The centre of Telford new town is on the left, near the site of the proposed Inter-City Telford Central Station, the construction of which has now been authorised. Beyond the new station site the train passes through a tunnel, then drops down to **Oakengates** station. The pit-mounds and other detritus of the Industrial Revolution look strangely attractive now that nature has provided a covering of heather, grasses and trees, but they do serve to remind us of the area's proud industrial past.

Approaching Wellington, at Stafford Junction, the former LNWR Stafford line comes in from the right; this only serves Donnington Ordnance Depot these days. From this junction, as far as Shrewsbury, the line was once jointly owned by the GWR and the LNWR. (Readers may recall memories of 'Kings' pulling their expresses away from Wellington Station up Tan Bank). **Wellington** has a fine station, dating from 1849, befitting the pleasant little town, which seems to be exceptionally busy on Market Days (Tuesdays, Thursdays & Saturdays).

The award-winning Ironbridge Gorge Museum complex can best be reached, if using public transport, from Wellington, but the visitor should spend a whole day there in order to appreciate its varied attractions to the full. The several museum sites are some distance apart and, though it is possible to walk between them, it would probably be better to spend the day by concentrating on either Blists Hill and Coalport, or Ironbridge and Coalbrookdale. Further information is available from the museum offices on Telford (0952) 453522. Note, bus services may be difficult.

The Iron Bridge, after which the village is named, is the highlight of the area for many visitors. It was the world's first iron bridge when built in 1779, by Abraham Darby III, and is still a marvellous sight, spanning the River Severn at a picturesque spot. At Coalbrookdale one can see the original furnace where Abraham Darby I invented the process of smelting iron ore with coke instead of charcoal, the technical breakthrough which is regarded as having sparked off the Industrial Revolution. At Blists Hill, amongst a whole range of attractions, including Victorian-style homes and shops, steam operated winding gear, and an inclined plane (once used to haul tub-boats up from the river), there are two preserved steam locomotives, including 49395, a former 0-8-0 of the LNWR, which is owned by the National Railway Museum.

As the train departs from Wellington, the trackbed of the former line to Nantwich can be seen on the right, whilst, high up on the left, the passenger has ample time to view The Wrekin, the famous 1,334 feet high hill whose summit affords spectacular views of neighbouring counties. It is a half-day walk to the top and back, the easiest way being past the golf club to Forest Glen, then past Heaven's Gate and Hell's Gate!

The train traverses the Shropshire Plain, past Allscott Sugar Works, now, sadly, disconnected from the railway network, then speeds Westwards, crossing the River Tern, the dried-up Shropshire Union Canal and the River Severn meandering across its flood plain. After a long cutting, the panorama of Shrewsbury comes into view, with the 11th century Abbey Foregate visible on the left.

SHREWSBURY

by Michael Shaw

Shrewsbury is set on a hill in a loop of the River Severn. The neck of the loop, being a good defensive position, is occupied by the castle. Close by is the railway station, a Tudor style building of 1848 with, unusually, another storey added below in 1902-3.

The town has been an important railway junction for more than a century and despite some closures still offers trains to Manchester, London, Cardiff, Swansea, Aberystwyth, Pwllheli and Chester.

Leaving the station, turn left and climb Castlegate towards the town centre. On the right is a building which was the grammar school (of 1590 and 1630) and which is now the library.

On the left is the castle, built in the mid 12th century on a Norman site. It has been much altered since and now houses a military museum.

Carry on to the top of the hill and in front of you is Pride Hill. This and the streets to the right form the towns main shopping area. To the left of Pride Hill is the part of the town which makes Shrewsbury distinctive. It is an area of small streets and alleys, parts of which are, mercifully, almost free from traffic. It contains the mediaeval church of St Mary and the Lady Chapel of Old St Chads. In addition there are two mediaeval church towers with 18th century naves (St Alkmunds in gothic style and St Julians in classical style; the latter is now used for secular purposes). The 18th century St Chads stands in a fine position overlooking the Quarry, the town's park. From here there are views over the river to the buildings of Shrewsbury Public School.

Also in the old town centre is the Clive House Museum (Clive of India lived here). It contains a good collection of local porcelain and the museum of the 1st Queens Dragoon Guards. For relics of Clive himself it is necessary to travel the 20 miles to Powis Castle just outside Welshpool.

Telford's Holyhead Road runs through the town and twice crosses the river. To the east is the English Bridge and to the west the Welsh Bridge. Over the English Bridge is Abbey Foregate and the Abbey which was begun in 1083, altered in the 15th century and again in 1862 and 1886.

Beyond, down Abbey Foregate, but visible from many parts of the town, is a Doric column to commemorate Lord Hill, a local hero at the battle of Waterloo.

Over the Welsh Bridge lies Frankwell with many half timbered buildings. Up the hill, past the traffic island, is Charles Darwin's birthplace, now occupied by Government offices.

Returning over the Welsh Bridge you come to Rowleys House museum of local history with a strong Roman section showing material from Viriconium which is located 5 miles to the east.

Shrewsbury has a lot to offer and is well worth visiting. For further information apply to the Tourist Information Office at the Music Hall in the square (phone: 0743 522019).

BIRMINGHAM — WALSALL
By Ken Russell

BIRMINGHAM NEW STREET

duddeston

ASTON

witton

perry barr

hamstead

bescot

WALSALL

The 11 mile rail route to Walsall has a fast half hourly electric train service which operates on weekdays. There is no Sunday service.

A description of the line from Birmingham New Street to Aston is included in the Birmingham-Lichfield lines article.

The route from Aston to Bescot runs through the Tame Valley and was opened by the Grand Junction Railway in 1837. Leaving Aston the Lichfield line leads off to the right weaving under the lofty viaducts at Spaghetti Junction where the Aston Expressway meets the M6 Motorway.

After the train passes beneath the Aston Expressway, Aston Parish Church is on the left, with the park beyond containing Aston Hall. Approaching **Witton** station on the right is the first view of the River Tame. On the left is Aston Villa Football Club stadium.

The line from Witton to **Perry Barr** is undistinguished. The unusual feature of Perry Barr Station is its name. There are many examples of stations being named after villages which were located miles from the station. It is suspected there are very few stations whose name was created by the original railway builders and has become the name of a district and a parliamentary constituency.

Perry Barr station was originally in the country at the point where the Grand Junction Railway crossed the Birmingham-Walsall Road. Perry was a village about a mile north of the station. Barr (originally misspelt until 1894 as Bar) was the name of the high ground to the north of Perry.

Today Perry Barr station serves the North Birmingham Polytechnic and a shopping centre which is currently being extended. Perry Park which is under a mile away is the site of the annual Birmingham Show and contains the Alexandra Athletics stadium, home of the famous Birchfield Harriers. Many international competitions are held here. To reach Perry Park and the stadium turn left leaving the station then walk along Walsall Road. An alternative to walking is to ride on the 51, 52 or 59 bus which runs frequently from the stops beyond the shopping centre.

On leaving Perry Barr the River Tame is again visible as we pass alongside playing fields. The train traverses the triangle junction which is the start of the Soho Loop line via Handsworth Park to Soho. On the hill to our left the Lea Hall mansion still overlooks the area but the Perry Hall after which the riverside park on the right was named has long since vanished leaving only a moat for use as a childrens boating facility.

Immediately after the train leaves a cutting it crosses the River Tame. This river

Birmingham — Walsall cont.

with its tributaries in industrial areas is heavily polluted, and the most polluted part is just here.

The next station is **Hamstead**. This station was opened in 1862 as Hamstead and Great Barr. Hamstead was a mining village adjacent to the station. Great Barr is the high ground to the north of the village and developed as a fashionable housing area which supplied commuter traffic to the railway. The residents of Great Barr did not wish to be associated with the adjacent mining village and in 1875 persuaded the railway company to re-name the station Great Barr. Such are the changes in fashion that the name has recently changed to Hamstead.

As the train leaves Hamstead, on the right is a housing development on the site of the colliery. The railway now passes through a green belt area known as the Sandwell Wedge. There are numerous views of the river with lakes and banks recently constructed by the Severn Trent Water Authority to control flooding and pollution. The Sandwell Wedge reaches well into the town of West Bromwich high on the hill. In the neighbourhood are opportunties for horse riding, sailing, wind surfing and walking.

The green of Sandwell Wedge comes to an abrupt end as the train passes under motorway viaducts at the Rea Hall interchange. To the right is the T junction of the M5 with the M6. The railway passes through housing estates, on the left is Charlemont Estate and on the right the historically named Bustleholm Mill Estate. The bridge conveniently linking both estates is surely a worthy site for a railway station. Immediately after the housing, the line goes under a high brick canal aqueduct dating from 1844, some 7 years after the railway was opened.

Bescot station is located at the far end of a marshalling yard alongside the M6 motorway and a locomotive depot. The station is an excellent viewing point, a trainspotters paradise, and the marshalling yards are an important cog in the Speedlink Freight Network.

At Bescot station the Grand Junction Line continues ahead towards Wolverhampton as the train turns right under the M6 viaduct and alongside the route built by the North Staffordshire Railway in 1847. The line from Dudley joins from the left and Fellow Park the ground of Walsall F.C. 'The Saddlers' is alongside the line on the same side. Next, at Pleck Junction the Walsall Power Signal Box is on our right.

The numerous junctions in the Bescot-Walsall area are for freight lines. Walsall was once the hub of 7 routes with passenger services to Dudley, Wolverhampton (2), Stafford, Lichfield and Birmingham via Bescot or Sutton Park. Walsall still has potential for restoring local passenger services to Wolverhampton, to Cannock, and possibly to the Dudley-Stourbridge route.

Walsall, population over ¼ million and the 13th largest town in the country has one of the best shopping centres in the conurbation. The street market held every day except Wednesday, Thursday and Sunday is well worth visiting, and is claimed to be the oldest street market in the country. A further attraction is that many of the shopping streets have been pedestrianised and it is planned to extend this in the future.

The station entrance is in a shopping centre known as the Saddlers Centre — commemorating the town's historical association with the leather industry. Walk straight ahead from the station entrance into Park Street where many national chain stores are located. For the market turn right into Park Street and go across

Portico entrance to Soho Foundry, Smethwick

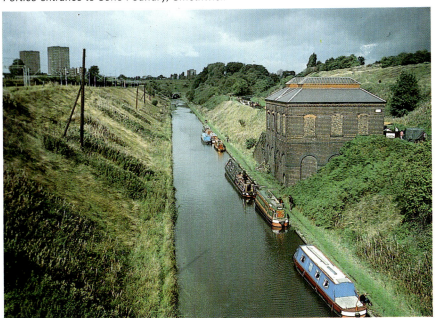

Narrow boat rally at Smethwick Rolfe Street. The engine house is between the lower Telford and higher Smeaton Canals

Birmingham — Walsall cont.

the pelican lights at Bridge Street. The market is straight ahead and it extends up the hill to St Matthews Parish Church. There is an interesting museum and Art Gallery next to the Town Hall in Lichfield Street.

Within a short distance of the town centre are the pleasant lakeside gardens of the Arboretum where the Walsall miniature steam railway is located. The railway operates over a ¼ mile double track main line at weekends and bank holidays from 2 p.m. Easter to October. The number 376 bus runs from the St Pauls bus station to the Arboretum. The St Pauls bus station is through the passage opposite the entrance to the Saddlers Centre.

The Willenhall Lock Museum is also located on the outskirts of the town. The number 529 bus is the most convenient to reach the museum, the journey taking 15 minutes. Ask to alight at Walsall Street. The 529 bus starts in Park Street, turn left at the entrance to the Saddlers Centre.

On the northern boundary of Walsall there is the large Chasewater Reservoir used for power boat racing and the adjacent Chasewater Light Railway which utilises a section of the former Midland Railway mineral line. Buses 345 or 385 from Walsall take about 40 minutes. Within only 20 minutes of central Walsall buses 376 and 377 can take visitors to the wide open vista of Barr Beacon (277m/ 700ft) which offers a panorama of Walsall, Sutton Park, North Birmingham, and much of the Black Country towards Dudley. Alight at the cross-roads and follow Beacon Road for 3 minutes to the well signed entrance to the Beacon.

LOCAL LINE SUPPORTERS

If you would like to keep informed about developments on your local rail line why not get in touch with a line supporters group. There are a number in the Midlands and details of some of them are given below:—

Redditch & Alvechurch Rail Users Association —
Mr. C. May, Foxlydiate Crescent, Batchley, Redditch, B97 6NS.
Wolverhampton Rail Supporters —
Mr. I. Jenkins, 283 Stafford Road, Oxley, Wolverhampton, WV10 6DQ.
Walsall Rail Supporters —
Mr. K. H. Russell, 38 Somerset Road, Rushall, Walsall, WS4 2DP.
N. Warwicks. Line Defence Committee —
Mr. F. S. Mayman, Shadwell House, Shadwell Street, Birmingham, B4 6LJ.
Cotswold Line Promotion Group —
Mr. A. S. Williams, 21 Trent Close, Droitwich, Worcs., WR9 8TH.
Birmingham, Kidderminster & Worcester Line Prom. Group —
Mr. J. Colley, 387 Hurcott Road, Kidderminster, Worcs.
Bromsgrove Passenger Action Group —
Mr. R. Swift, 7 Blenheim Avenue, Bromsgrove, Worcs.
Lichfield Rail Action Group —
Mr. D. Woodcock, 20 Oak Road, Barton under Needwood, Staffs., DE13 8LR.
Matlock — Sinfin Rail Users Group —
Mr. S. Hartropp, 72 Empress Road, Derby, DE3 6TE
Stratford on Avon Rail Campaign —
Mr. D. Goodman, 12 Blue Cap Road, Stratford on Avon.

BIRMINGHAM — LEICESTER

by Clive Rathbone

BIRMINGHAM NEW STREET
|
water orton
|
NUNEATON
|
hinckley
|
narborough
|
LEICESTER

The hourly service is provided partly by locomotive hauled trains which are travelling to destinations further afield and by diesel multiple unit railcars, most of which terminate at Leicester, providing an hourly service from New Street Station.

Emerging from New Street South tunnel the train traverses the points at Proof House Junction. For a few yards it travels alongside the London to Birmingham line before diving down the side of a viaduct to pass beneath it and to gain its own route which was part of the Midland Railway, originally the Derby and Birmingham Junction opened in 1842.

For the first five miles the train passes through a landscape which is heavily industrialised. After passing the Aston to Stechford line, on the right hand side is the works of Metro Cammell which has been associated with the building of railway rolling stock for generations. There is a fair chance that the carriage in which you are travelling was built here. Look on the doorstep as you alight and you may see the name of this world famous firm. They are the builders of most of the trains running on the London Underground and those for the brand new Tyne and Wear Metro. Overseas, amongst many others, they were responsible for the rolling stock for the Hong Kong Rapid Transit system and coming right back to their own doorstep for the cars on the revolutionary Maglev system at Birmingham International Airport.

Soon, beyond the marshalling yards, can be seen for the first time the M6 motorway on the left. This motorway viaduct which is almost 2 miles long was said to be the longest in England when it was opened in 1972. The train maintains a good speed over this section as the line is straight. On the left hand side is much derelict land and it seems odd that developers keep taking over green fields when here there is acre upon acre of land ripe for re-development.

On the left after passing Fort Dunlop and passing under the Chester Road, Castle Vale comes into view. There used to be a station, Castle Bromwich, here but it no longer exists having been closed before the housing developments, which seems a great pity as it would now clearly have a vast potential.

A mere five miles from New Street and the train crosses the boundary of the West Midlands County into Warwickshire and the scenery becomes rural with the river Tame, one of the districts "major" rivers, on the right. **Water Orton** is the first station which, apart from one mid-day service, is now served by peak hour trains only. Immediately after passing Water Orton the line to Derby diverges to the left and we take the right hand fork towards Nuneaton.

The journey continues through the level Tame Valley with Hams Hall power station on the left. Immediately before the train takes the right hand line at

Inter City train passed Telford's "Galton" bridge, Smethwick

Charles Darwin statue, Shrewsbury
Photo by courtesy of The Heart of England Tourist Board

The Roman "Jewry" wall and St. Nicholas Church, Leicester

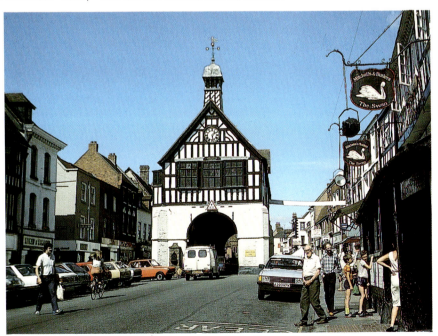

Bridgnorth — the market town and terminus of The Severn Valley Railway

Birmingham — Leicester cont.

Whitacre Junction on the right are the waterworks of the River Blyth. The cathedral-like proportions of the old steam pumping engine house are worth noting. From Whitacre the line climbs to Arley through typical Warwickshire scenery, not dramatic but in places heavily wooded and seen most effectively in spring, autumn and fresh winter mornings.

The train emerges from Arley tunnel to descend through the outskirts of **Nuneaton** to Trent Valley station. This station is on the electrified West Coast Main Line from London to Glasgow and is served by Inter-City trains and is also the terminus for local trains from Stafford. Trent Valley is one of those stations where non-stop trains pass at full speed — often in excess of 100 m.p.h.

Nuneaton is best known as the birthplace of George Elliot (Mary Ann Evans). She was born at South Farm, Arbury (not open to the public) which lies in the grounds of Arbury Hall, home of the Newdegate family since 1586. Arbury is a Gothic style building with a Georgian interior containing period furniture and memorabilia of George Elliot. It has fine gardens and stables with displays of old bicycles and farm implements. Arbury can be reached easily by Midland Red bus No. 39 which leaves from the bus station.

The bus station is situated a short distance from Trent Valley station. Walk along Bond Street, turn right into New Town Road and the bus station is on the left. The town centre is quite near to the railway station and to reach it proceed through the bus station. Here is the town's Museum and Art Gallery to which admission is free and where more memorabilia of George Elliot can be seen.

Tourist Information can be obtained from the Library, telephone Nuneaton 384027.

Leaving Nuneaton the Leicester route curves sharply to the left away from the West Coast Main Line. In a short distance a line joins from the left which allows trains, usually freight, from the Birmingham direction to continue to Leicester without having to negotiate the complicated junctions at Nuneaton station and without conflict with W.C.M.L. trains.

The next station is in Leicestershire at the small industrial town of **Hinckley**. The town is noted for its association with the hosiery and shoe industries. It will probably see many additional visitors in 1985 as it is the 500th anniversary of the death of King Richard III. The King met his death at Bosworth field in 1485 during the last important battle in the wars of the Roses. Bosworth field is 5 miles from Hinckley. For tourist information telephone Hinckley 30852 or 635106.

Narborough is the next station which is a suburb of Leicester from which many workers commute into that city. After crossing the River Soar the train

Birmingham — Leicester cont.

approaches Wigston where Leicester County Council is preparing to open a new station, possible in 1985. At Wigston North Junction our train joins the Midland main line from London, St Pancras, for the last three miles into Leicester.

From **Leicester** connections can be made to permit travel by rail to places such as Melton Mowbray, Market Harborough, Loughborough and East Anglia.

Leicester

Leicester is a fastincating city with numerous museums and a modern shopping centre. Although only raised to the status of a city in 1919 its history and some of its surviving buildings go back to the Roman era. Various museums illustrate the development of the city.

The Roman period is shown in the Jewry Wall museum. The exhibits include mosaics and a substantial wall. St Nicholas's church, which is adjacent, is one of the oldest churches in England. It is Saxon in style and may have been built in the 7th century. The church was partly constructed with bricks from Roman buildings.

Leicester Castle is near the Jewry Wall museum. Little masonry remains from the Saxon and Norman castle but the 12th century building is concealed within 18th century brickwork and is now used for the Crown Court.

The construction of the Castle Church (St. Mary de Castro) was begun in 1107 and continued for 200 years. Near the altar are five stone seats for the clergy dating from 1180. They are regarded as the finest examples in England.

Simon-de-Montfort, leader of the revolt of the Barons against Henry III and Cardinal Wolsey who died at Leicester Abbey in 1530 are two notable figures from history associated with the city.

Other museums are devoted to costumes, the Leicestershire Regiment and social history. The Museum of Technology has a fine collection of hosiery machinery, horse drawn vehicles and an 86 ton steam shovel all housed around four beam pumping engines which are steamed regularly.

The Tourist Information Office, open normal hours on weekdays, is only 600 yards from the station. Turn right into London Road and follow its continuation named Granby Street to the main Post Office. Turn left into Bishop Street and the information office is on the left.

Leawood pump house, near Cromford

Horse drawn barge on the Cromford Canal

BIRMINGHAM — DERBY — MATLOCK

by Alan Bevan

BIRMINGHAM NEW STREET
|
water orton
|
wilnecote
|
TAMWORTH
|
BURTON ON TRENT
|
peartree
|
DERBY
|
duffield
|
belper
|
ambergate
|
WHATSTANDWELL
|
CROMFORD
|
MATLOCK BATH
|
MATLOCK

To avoid steep gradients railways often follow river valleys and this route is no exception. In the journey from Birmingham city centre to the Derbyshire hills the railway follows the rivers Tame, Trent and Derwent.

The Birmingham — Derby line has a frequent service with a wide variety of trains from Inter City 125's to diesel railcars on the local services. The Derby — Matlock local trains are usually operated by the new "sprinter" vehicles on a regular interval service with good connections at Derby.

The route from Birmingham New Street to Water Orton is described in the Birmingham — Leicester article.

Immediately after **Water Orton** station the line forks left away from the Leicester route. After passing under the M42 and over the River Tame the cooling towers of Hams Hall power station will be noted. Next come flat riverside meadows where former sand and gravel excavations have been converted into a series of lakes for river improvements and leisure purposes.

Kingsbury village is ahead on the left with an oil terminal and colliery sidings on the right. Beyond the M42 extension there are further excavations associated with brick and tile manufacture before the train passes new housing developments adjacent to **Wilnecote,** the next local station.

The train now approaches the much expanded town of **Tamworth.** The line crosses a viaduct over the River Anker, a tributary of the River Tame which it joins to the left. Tamworth, once the capital of the Kingdom of Mercia, is still dominated by its Norman castle. Just half a mile from the station there is a bustling town with an indoor shopping centre; the castle museum and grounds (open 10-5 Mon.-Thurs. and Sat., plus 2-5 Sun.) and indoor and outdoor swimming pool; and an interesting elevated town hall in the middle of Market Street. Visit also the statue of Robert Peel, founder of the Peelers — the original police force. Immediately beneath the high level station is the electrified main line from London Euston to Glasgow.

Beyond Tamworth the train runs into rural Staffordshire and enters the flood plain where there is the confluence of three rivers. The Mease comes first on the right then the railway crosses the Tame, and the Trent, all merging to the right just

Birmingham — Derby — Matlock cont.

before Wychnor Junction. Following the course of the River Trent the Drakelow power station is on the right before reaching the famous brewery town of **Burton on Trent.**

Here visitors can enjoy the Bass Museum of brewing history in Horninglow Street which is open 11-4.30 every day for adults and children alike. Audio visuals, posters, models and tape recordings all help to bring the colourful history of this tipsy industry to life. Exhibits relate to road, river, canal, horse, and railway transport and samples of the brew can be consumed in the bar or beer garden.

Beyond Burton the railway passes through flat but pleasant countryside. The River Dove is soon crossed, The Trent and Mersey Canal runs alongside the railway and the line from Stoke on Trent joins from the left. Willington power station is on the right as the train approaches the outskirts of Derby. The branch to Sinfin joins on the right immediately before **Peartree** station. The branch and station have recently re-opened for commuter traffic to local industries.

The train soon enters **Derby** station. The variety of rolling stock to the right is where British Rail have their research and engineering works. Derby was, of course, the headquarters of the former Midland Railway Company. Visitors can make for a glassworks to watch craftsmen produce lead crystal glassware by hand and to buy some products. Derwent Crystals is in Little Bridge Street off Bridge Street and is open 9-5 Mon.-Sat. The City of Derby also offers an Art Gallery, Museums, the world famous Crown Porcelain Works, good shops and restaurants and a Cathedral.

For the Matlock Valley line it is necessary to change trains at Derby. Leaving Derby station the substantial tower of Derby Cathedral can be seen on the left as the train crosses the River Derwent. The train now proceeds through the Derwent Valley. At first the valley is wide but soon the famous Derbyshire hills begin to close in approaching the railway as the valley becomes narrower. **Duffield** and **Belper** stations are passed before the train approaches Ambergate Junction where there is a fine view of the river on the left.

The Matlock Valley branch line begins at Ambergate Junction where the Matlock train branches left. The main line to the right is used by Derby — Chesterfield Inter City trains. The principal attractions of the Matlock Valley are the National Tramway Museum, the Cromford Canal, The Arkwright Mill and some very attractive countryside. The stations are conveniently situated to give easy access to all these attractions and it is possible to walk the short distances between the stations.

Ambergate is the first station and the next station, **Whatstandwell,** is the station for the National Tramway Museum. Allow at least three hours for this excursion. The museum is less than a mile from the station at Crich in the hill top quarry beneath the monument. Leave the station by the footbridge, turn right at the road then left up a narrow steep hill through Crich Carr. After the walk you will enjoy riding on one of the 40 preserved tram cars and sampling the museum's refreshment facilities.

After a tunnel and splendid riverside views the train enters **Cromford** station. The principal interests here are the various buildings associated with the industrialist Sir Richard Arkwright, and the canal. Leave the station and walk towards the village; on the right is the drive to Willersley Castle which was built

Glasgow tram at The National Tramway Museum

Birmingham — Derby — Matlock cont.

by Arkwright. Now owned by the Methodist Guild, the house was not completed until after his death. Next cross the river, on the left is a picnic area and the Cromford Canal. A little further on the right is the original Arkwright Mill which is open to the public. Beyond the mill cross the A6 into the village where there is an excellent inn.

During the afternoon of summer Saturdays and Sundays the Cromford Canal Society operates a horse drawn barge service to Leawood. The horse barge, which is a little quicker than walking, terminates between the steam museum at the beginning of the dismantled Cromford and High Peak Railway and Leawood pumping house. The Pumphouse contains an 1849 beam engine with pump and locomotive boilers which were supplied by the Midland Railway in 1900. The pump is steamed occasionally during the summer. Phone 062982 3727 for the dates of this together with working days at the steam museum. Leawood pumping station is just under half way between Cromford and Whatstandwell stations so there is a simple choice of returning to Cromford or walking alongside the dried up canal to Whatstandwell.

If we decide to stay on the train it enters another tunnel and emerges at **Matlock Bath** where there are lots of amusement areas, cafes, and shops along the main road and riverside. An intersting Mining Museum is next to the fish ponds and the Petrifying Well. A new cable car facility takes visitors across the valley and up to the Tree Tops Centre and restaurant on the Heights of Abraham. Also on offer is the Great Rutland Cavern, the Nestus Mine and the Prospect Tower for really panoramic views of the Derbyshire Peak District. A little further up the gorge by train, bus, or walk is the main town of **Matlock** which is the centre for shopping, markets, bus station, and riverside gardens. Riber Castle, now a ruin, can be seen on a hill top where a wildlife park is open to the public. At the rail station there is the Peak Railway Society's Steam Centre with exhibits, bookshop and cafe.

In addition to the train there is a regular bus service which operates between Matlock, Cromford, the Tramway Museum at Crich and the Midland Railway Centre near Ripley.

BIRMINGHAM CITY CENTRE
by Frank Hastilow

Nearly all the excursions described in this little book start from Birmingham. It does not seem out of place therefore to devote a little space to describing very briefly something of what present day Birmingham has to offer.

A LITTLE HISTORY

In 1166 a market was granted to Peter de Bermingham for the sale of livestock probably the first formal recognition of the trading potential of the place. Because of the local topography most of the local trade routes passed through, or very close to, Birmingham and this seems to have been the prime reason for establishing the market.

The town benefitted from this and we find about this time evidence of the rebuilding of St. Martins, the parish church of Birmingham. Throughout all the centuries there are four recumbent stone figures which have held a place in this church. One of them, an effigy of a William de Bermingham, is considered to be the oldest object fashioned by man in the city. All are probably members of the de Bermingham family although their exact identity is uncertain. William's shield carries the bend dexter of five lozenges which is today incorporated in the arms of the modern city.

The great development of Birmingham though took place in Victorian times.

The re-development craze of the 1960s destroyed many interesting and pleasant buildings and replaced them with modern and in many cases characterless, concrete erections. This was the time also when the inner ring road, now Queensway, was built which has since had such a constricting influence on any expansion of the city centre, besides sending pedestrians underground in many places.

MODERN BIRMINGHAM

Despite the re-development of the 1960s there are still many reminders of the Victorian era. Victoria Square is the central focus, dominated by a statue of Queen Victoria.

On one side of the square is the Town Hall completed in 1850 and based on the temple of Castor and Pollux in Rome. Facing the Queen is the Head Post Office, recently renovated some would say with too much veneration for Victoriana.

Behind the Queen is the vast bulk of the Council house built in 1874-79 and itself a fine example of Victorian architecture, built in Italian Renaissance style. An extension of the Council House houses the city Museum and Art Gallery which is referred to in more detail later.

Outside the Art Gallery is Chamberlain Square with its fountain which, in one form or another, has long been a feature of central Birmingham. It was built to commemorate the Chamberlain family whose civic activities earned for Birmingham the reputation of being (in those days) the 'best governed city in the world'. Also in Chamberlain Square are statues of two other famous men associated with the city — Joseph Priestley and James Watt. Slightly above Chamberlain Square is the modern Central Library which includes the usual lending and reference sections. It also houses an internationally renowned extensive Shakespeare Library.

A little way away, on the corner of Broad Street is the Hall of Memory, built to

Birmingham City Centre cont.

commemorate the city's dead of two world wars. Standing a little further back is Baskerville House, designed to house some of the city administration and named after another well known man of Birmingham, whose printing works at one time occupied this site. A little further along Broad Street is the Birmingham Repertory Theatre, successor to the one in Station Street founded by Sir Barry Jackson. The original, by the way, is still in use as a theatre, housing amateur productions. On the other side of Broad Street, outside the Registry Office, is a memorial to Boulton, Murdoch and Watt, all associated with the Soho Foundry and the construction of early steam engines.

Continuing along Broad Street towards Five Ways, have a look at Gas Street Basin with its canals and narrow boats. Birmingham is at the centre of the country's canal network which helped its prosperity in an earlier age. It is said to have more canals than Venice. You will also pass names like Brasshouse Passage which marks the site of the earliest venture into actual metal making in the city.

BIRMINGHAM CATHEDRAL

Birmingham Cathedral, while clearly not the equal of the great historic cathedrals of, for example, Lichfield or Gloucester, is worthy of a visit in its own right. Standing between Colmore Row and Temple Row the open space surrounding it is the largest in the city centre and is much valued for this reason.

The church itself was consecrated in 1715 and was designed by a local architect, Thomas Archer. His building had something in common with the works of Wren and Vanburgh but was by no means merely imitative having considerable merits of its own.

Built in the Palladian style it is one of the country's classic examples of English Baroque architecture. Four of the windows were designed by Sir Edward Burne-Jones who was in fact baptised at St. Philips. When the diocese of Birmingham was formed in 1905 St. Philips was designated as the cathedral.

An extensive programme of restoration and improvement has recently been completed and the whole of the interior splendidly re-decorated in English early 18th century style.

The excellent acoustics of Archer's building cause it to be much used in the service of music and the arts in addition to its regular relngous functions.

SHOPPING

Most shopping facilities, which include major department stores such as Lewis's and Rackhams, and larger branches of the usual chain stores are located in the Corporation Street, New Street, High Street area although one or two good class shops are situated in Broad Street, as is H.M.S.O. (which is well worth a visit).

The markets are located in the Bull Ring adjacent to St. Martins church. This can be reached by turning right at the top of the escalator from New Street station and walking through the Birmingham and Bull Ring shopping centres.

Another place worth visiting is the Great Western Arcade, newly restored to something approaching its Victorian splendour at considerable cost. This arcade, as its name suggests, was the first approach to the city centre which passengers encountered when leaving the, now defunct, main line Snow Hill station (shortly to be re-built as a station for commuters).

Birmingham City Centre cont.

THE ARTS
Theatres

Birmingham is one of the major theatre centres outside London and the recently re-built Hippodrome is capable of taking the largest productions, musicals or ballet. The Alexandra is a smaller theatre and presents a programme of more intimate productions. The Birmingham Repertory Theatre in Broad Street usually provides more adventurous plays with a leavening of classics. There is also a theatre restaurant, the Night Out, in the Horsefair, which provides a night club atmosphere and with top line entertainers. There are also several cinemas.

MUSEUMS

As referred to earlier, the City Museum and Art Gallery occupies a central position in Chamerlain Square, just off Victoria Square and admission is free. The Museum contains much of interest in connection with local industries, some of which are now extinct. There is a splendid collection of local work in precious metals. The Natural History Section is worth seeing as are many other sections.

The Art Gallery, housed in the same building, has a large collection of paintings, particularly by the pre-Raphaelities, but including works by other world famous artists such as Tintoretto, Canalleto etc.

Not very far away in Newhall Street, is the Museum of Science and Industry. The main part of this museum, the Engineering Hall, was once a workshop of Elkington and Co. Ltd., an electro-plating firm which was founded in 1840. The star attraction for rail fans though is the Stanier Pacific "City" of Birmingham" around which, in fact, the Locomotive Hall was built. There are many other steam engines both mobile and static. The latter includes the newly restored beam pumping engine, built by James Watt in 1779 and believed to be the oldest steam engine in the world still in working order. Also relating to rail is the sole remaining Birmingham Corporation tramcar.

There are many other sections of the museum including those devoted to machine tools, aircraft and small arms — very much a local industry. The motor section has on display the Cobb — Railton special which once held the land speed record. The science section has a model of a nuclear reactor. Admission is free and the museum is open from 10 am to 5 pm Monday to Friday, 10 am to 5.30 on Saturdays and 2 pm to 5.30 pm on Sundays.

A number of engines in the Engineering Hall are run every day, powered by electric motors. Suitable ones, including the 1779 Watt engine are run on live steam, normally on the first and third Wednesdays in each month and for one weekend in March, May and October. Details of times and dates can be obtained by phoning 021-236 1022. Before leaving Newhall Street note on the opposite side of the road the Birmingham Assay Office on the corner of Charlotte Street. The Centrebus (service 101) is useful in getting to the Museum of Science and Industry — alight in Great Charles Street Queensway at Newhall Street.

Before leaving the Newhall Street area altogether it is worthwhile for those with an interest in the Great Western Railway and the old Snow Hill station to take a walk down Great Charles Street to St. Chads Circus (named after the Roman Catholic Cathedral nearby) and see the mural mosaics depicting aspects from the past of the G.W.R.

Birmingham City Centre cont.

MUSIC

The Town Hall is the home base of the City of Birmingham Symphony Orchestra which, under its chief conductor, Simon Rattle, is acquiring an international reputation amongst professional orchestras.

Free lunchtime organ recitals are normally given every Wednesday in the Town Hall on the magnificent and recently rebuilt organ.

Regular concerts and recitals also take place in the Cathedral and the Midland Institute.

ACCESS

New Street station is in the centre of Birmingham. Escalators link the concourse with the Birmingham Shopping Centre which in turn is linked to the Bull Ring. Descending the ramp from the shopping centre brings one directly into New Street at the top of which (turning to the left) is Victoria Square. A little to the right, at the bottom of the ramp, is a stop for the Centrebus (service 101) which circles the city centre at 5 minute intervals from 7 am to 6 pm on Mondays to Saturdays (there is no service on Bank Holiday Mondays). It is a very useful way of getting about in the central area.

Most of the trains from the Leamington, Solihull and North Warwick lines terminate at Moor Street station situated on Moor Street Ringway. It is but a short distance from New Street station and the direction is well signposted. There is a Centrebus stop close to the exit from the station.

A Tourist Information Centre and Ticket Shop (where bookings can be made for most entertainments in the city and at the National Exhibition Centre) is located in the City Arcade in Union Street. "Whats On" is published fortnightly by the Birmingham Convention and Visitor Bureau and is available free from many points in the city centre, including the Tourist Information Centre and is a mine of information about forthcoming events.

FURTHER READING

The following books and articles can be recommended to anyone who would like to delve a little deeper into what the Midlands can offer.

1. *"Railways of the West Midlands, A Chronology 1808 to 1954"*
Stephenson Locomotive Society, 1954

2. *"Regional History of the Railways of Great Britain"* Vol. 7 *"The West Midlands"*
David & Charles, 1973.

3. *"A History of Birmingham"* Vols. 1 & 2.
Oxford University Press, 1952

4. *"Places to Visit"*
Heart of England Tourist Board. 95p.

This little book is a mine of information and can be obtained from most booksellers.

64

THE RAILWAY DEVELOPMENT SOCIETY

The Railway Development Society seeks to improve rail services and promote the development of railways in this country. The National Society issues free to members a quarterly paper "Railway Development News" and a report on railway matters which are debated in Parliament.

The Society has branches throughout the country. The Midland Branch, the publishers of this book also issue a quarterly newsletter on Midland railway developments which is distributed free to Branch members.

The Midland Branch has in recent years successfully lobbied for the re-instatement of Snow Hill station in Birmingham and a new station at Telford. The Branch's current objectives include the development of the Birmingham — Henley in Arden — Stratford on Avon line, the introduction of a Walsall to Cannock local passenger service and the electrification of the Stourbridge, Solihull and Cross City lines.

Hednesford station has been closed for almost 20 years yet on three occasions in 1984 the station was packed with passengers. This was when the Midland Branch ran special trains to Portsmouth, York and Kidderminster. This was a practical demonstration of the Railway Development Society promoting rail usage and opening freight lines to passenger trains.

If you are interested in seeing the railways improved and receiving news of Railway developments WHY NOT JOIN US?

JOIN THE RAILWAY DEVELOPMENT SOCIETY

Subscription rates are as follows:—

Ordinary Members	£6
Corporate Members	£6
Students	£3
Pensioners (over 65)	£3
Family Membership	£5 + £1 for each additional member of family

Applications or enquiries should be sent to: Mr. F. J. Hastilow, 21 Norfolk Road Sutton Coldfield, West Midlands, B75 6SQ.

INDEX

Back Cover Photo: British Camp, Malvern